YOU, ME &

Everyone

WE KNOW

EVERYDAY ADVENTURES
IN MENTAL HEALTH

The History Press

First published 2014

The History Press Ireland
50 City Quay
Dublin 2
Ireland
www.thehistorypress.ie

British Library Cataloguing in Publication Data.
A catalogue record for this book is available from the British Library.

ISBN 978 1 84588 809 1

Typesetting and origination by The History Press

CONTENTS

FOREWORD

Growing up I never really understood the concept of mental health. For me the cosy mantra of 'it will be grand' put any problem to rest. At 18 this simple technique failed me. When a close friend told me they were suffering from depression, I didn't know how to react. Turning scared to the internet, I stumbled upon ReachOut.com. Their service helped me to understand what my friend was going through and how I could help. After facing this unknown world, I decided that I didn't want any young person anywhere going through this without support. I joined the ReachOut.com Youth Ambassador programme in the hope of taking the mystery out of mental health for other young people.

The ReachOut.com philosophy is that mental health is something all of us have all of the time. Everybody will have their own adventures in mental health and these will be different for all of us. For me, ReachOut.com has been the perfect online resource. Whenever I felt confused, scared or lost, I always knew I had somewhere to turn to. It's allowed me to realise that none of us are alone and everyone shares the same concerns.

This collection of stories helps show the whole spectrum of mental health. Perhaps you can identify with a certain line, quote or feeling. Perhaps you've been exactly where one of our writers has been, and hearing how they overcame a tough time will help. Perhaps you could never imagine experiencing some of situations described in this book, but gaining an insight into the lives of others will benefit you, providing the skills you need to empathise with another person's journey. If nothing else, I promise this book will illustrate that mental health is not a mysterious concept. Rather, it is the very act of living as experienced by you, me and everyone we know.

We all lead different journeys. From celebrities to students, mental health workers and sports stars, this book illustrates beautifully the concept of mental health as a shared human experience. So, share this book! Share the adventures, and your own. Life is a series of unexpected adventures, and sharing them is guaranteed to lighten the load.

Carmel Sayers, 2014

COMPASSION

'You have things to offer that nobody else does and the world needs these things.'

Melissa Carton-Mckevitt

Elaine Crowley

First and foremost, be kind to yourself. You may feel like the world is grey, and you are blending into it.

Try to remember there are people who love you. There are people who like you. And if you have difficulty liking yourself, ask those people why they want you in their life. If you cannot see the good in you, a good friend will point it out.

Should. Shouldn't. They are the worst words in the English language. How many times have you said to yourself, 'I should be happy. There's nothing wrong with my life. I shouldn't feel so low and so depressed. I have a family that loves me. I have food and shelter. I have a job/friends/every possession I could need. I shouldn't feel this way'?

You know what? You're entitled to feel any way you want. Eliminate those words from your vocabulary. It's hard to do. But try. Notice how you feel every time you try to tell yourself what you *should* and *should not* be feeling.

Everything in life is relative. A car breaking down, or an overdue bill, may be a simple matter to some. To others it can be a crippling blow. You feel the way you feel and that's that. End of.

I saw a picture of myself recently. I was 3 or 4 years old, belly laughing at the camera, without a care in the world. Looking at that picture broke my heart, because I know now that little girl had fairly difficult times ahead.

Yes, there were times I thought I'd never genuinely laugh again, there were times I didn't get out of bed for days, there were unkind words with friends I've since lost due to the utter misery and selfishness that depression can induce.

But you know what? There are good times too, great times, bloody fantastic times – and don't forget it.

When you're stuck in a rut it's hard to see a way out. But there is *always* a way out. It's not easy, there are no quick fixes but you'll get there. You will belly laugh again!

So start with the little things. Talk to someone you like. Get some fresh air and exercise. Avoid those who drag you down. Take baby steps.

It may take a while but you'll get there.

Be kind to yourself.

Melissa Maria Carton

I was 15 years old when I read a letter Gwen Stefani had written to her younger self. It had me at a loss. How could a strong, confident woman like her ever have felt as I have? Surely she always knew she was beautiful and talented? I bet she was never stood up for a date, never had someone make fun of the way she looked, never had anyone tell her she was worthless.

Back then I couldn't understand how she had ever felt insecure. Now, in my mid-twenties, I get it. I think back to my teen years, read my old diaries, pull out photographs I'd hidden, and I understand her perfectly. You couldn't have convinced 'teenage me' that it was all going to get better; that I wouldn't always feel so alone, so ugly, so insignificant. There has been a huge surge in the number of teenage suicides in recent years. So, from someone who has made it to the other side, let me share some advice I would give to my younger self – if only it had been possible!

You won't always be alone

Right now you feel desperately alone. You feel that if you try to connect with anyone they will just laugh at you. It cuts you up inside that you don't have friends and even though you try to convince yourself that you're better off alone, the truth is that you want someone to talk to. You believe that nobody wants you around and that you deserve all the nasty comments people make about you – but you don't. You will find friends. It may seem like you never will, but they're out there. Don't cut yourself off from the world. Your existence matters. You have things to offer that nobody else does, and the world needs these things. Once you allow yourself to shine you'll attract the right people to you. You have so much to give. Don't hide it all away.

Your friends do want to be around you

You've spent so long having people bully you and put you down that your trust has been dashed, but trust in this: your friends do want to be around you. You may think they involve you because they feel sorry for you. Maybe you even believe that they laugh about you behind your back – sure, who would really want to hang out with you? They're just hanging out with you to make themselves look better because you're such a loser, right? Wrong! They 100 per cent give a damn about you. They hang out with you because they see in you what even you can't see sometimes, that you're kind of, sort of, pretty awesome when you give yourself the chance. And do you know what? They'll still be your friends when you're in your twenties. They'll see you through all your ups and downs and you'll see them through theirs. They're wonderful, compassionate people who will always be there when you need them. What's more, they feel as lucky to have you as you feel to have them.

You are not now, nor have you ever been, ugly

Stop hiding from your reflection and other people. You are not ugly. You don't need to wear three layers of clothes or keep your head down so no one will look at you. Stop being ashamed of your body. You do not look too skinny. You do not look like a boy. You don't need to force-feed yourself. Your curves will come in their own time. You are not too short, you are not the 'plain' one in your group, you are not the most unattractive girl in every room. Right now you wish you looked like someone else. Don't! You are everything you need to be and more.

Don't determine your value by how a boy treats you

You're young and self-conscious and one thing you should never do is weigh up how much to value yourself based on the opinion of others. Relationships will come and go, but self-esteem is for keeps so don't tie yours to one person. It may seem like nothing when you dye your hair because your boyfriend prefers brunettes, or when you start ditching your hobbies and replacing them with his interests, but the fact of the matter is that anyone who truly loves you loves you for who you are and they would never want you to change. You would never expect anyone to change who they are for you, so why should they expect you to do a one-eighty on your dreams for them? You don't deserve to be put down, nor do you deserve to have someone yell into your face, to be hurt verbally or physically, or to be cheated on.

You don't need false friends hanging around, telling you it's your fault and if you just did as you were told he wouldn't lay into you. You didn't have it coming when he grabbed you by the throat during an argument and you shouldn't have had to apologise to him afterwards for making him do it. You know deep down you're better than that and some day this knowledge will come to the surface. It can take a long time to step away from an abusive relationship and realise it wasn't your fault. You might think it was all in your head, or that you overreacted. When you get far enough away from it, you will look back on what happened and see how it affected the people around you who really care for you. You will see how worried they were for your well-being and you'll know you never should have let anyone treat you like that. We can't change the past, but we can learn from it.

There is someone better for you out there – someone who will never tell you how you should look, who you should see or what you should do with your life; someone who will support you in whatever you want to do and always put you first; and, more importantly, someone who will respect you, because you are worthy of being respected and that is something you should never forget.

You are not stupid

The only unintelligent thing you've ever done is tell yourself that you were dumb. You might feel that because you're not doing a master's at university, or because you didn't study what people wanted you to study in college, that you're a let-down or unaccomplished. Ask yourself: 'Who has made me feel stupid?' Then ask yourself: 'What makes them so much better than me that they are entitled to make me feel stupid?' I think you'll find that nothing entitles them to make you feel that way, and that you've never been in the least bit stupid. You are clever and always have been. You have to know that.

Everyone around you values your opinion and they do so because they consider you knowledgeable. So know that yourself. After all, believing in yourself is probably the smartest thing you'll ever do.

Don't give up:
you've no idea what you're about to accomplish

None of us can see the road ahead of us, but believe me it is bright and it always will be. Life will throw you curve-balls. There are things that you won't be able to control and there will be dark days that you won't want to face up to but I implore you: don't give up. It's one of the hardest things to admit but several times in my teens I wanted to kill myself and every day I live I'm glad I didn't. I look back on all the things I've accomplished and think, 'If I had gone through with it back then I never would have done any of this'. You have no idea of the things that are coming your way: the things you'll do, the places you'll see, the people you'll meet. Those dark days don't last forever and we can never let ourselves become a victim of them. You must learn to take the power in a powerless situation and never let that situation have power over you. You will do things in these next couple of years that most people won't do in an entire lifetime. Your life is important. Your life plays a crucial part in the lives of others and if you ceased to exist a part of them would too. An entire life, created by you, would never have been present in this world if you had given up. You happened for a reason; there are no accidents in nature. Even if the road is bumpy, even if you didn't get off to the best start, even if the direction seems unclear, your life is going somewhere. You will inspire others, you will help those who need it most, you will save someone's life, but first, you have to save your-self. Believe in yourself, know that your life has great worth and that you are everything that you need to be.

Never give up on yourself and your possibilities are infinite. Choose to fight and you will win

Don't give up – you've no idea what you are about to accomplish.

Louise O'Neill

I had been planning my escape from my small town for most of my teen years. When I turned 18, I was going to leave. When I turned 18, I was going to move to Dublin and never look back. I was going to study English at TCD, I was going to be popular, and I was going to feel good about myself, and I was going to feel happy. When I turned 18, everything was going to be different.

And here I was, finally, living in Trinity Halls. I had made it.

I left my apartment the first day, got the bus into town and even that was a bit of an adventure as I was used to driving everywhere at home. The bus driver dropped me off by Stephen's Green shopping centre and it took me almost two hours to find Trinity College, such was my unfamiliarity with the city centre. My feelings of disorientation didn't end there. I felt *wrong* – my accent, where I was from, the clothes I was wearing – everything about me just felt as if it marked me out as somehow not fitting in with my classmates. I held my tongue in tutorials as others boldly stated their opinions, afraid that if I opened my mouth to speak I would betray how very wrong I really was. I was used to being the best in my English classes, the brightest, and I didn't like this new role I found myself playing. I missed one class, then another, then a week of classes, then a month.

'Are you still enrolled here?' a tutor asked me in surprise as I traipsed into the exam hall at the end of term. 'I thought you had dropped out.'

No. I hadn't dropped out. I had spent the first year of university hiding away in my bedroom, refusing to go back to Clonakilty at the weekends in case anyone at home would think I had 'failed'. I knew that everyone else must be having the time of their lives, partying like they were sorority girls in a Hollywood movie, making friends that would end up being their bridesmaids, meeting boys that would end up being their husbands. I felt so ashamed at my inability to join in that I lied, made up stories of debauchery and fun to tell friends at home so they wouldn't know what a complete loser I had become.

It's funny looking back at that time now. I do wonder what would have happened if I had been brave enough to join the drama society, if I had auditioned for that play, if I had admitted that I felt a bit lost and asked for help. I bet that if I had tried to be more honest other people might have admitted that they felt a little lost as well, that their college experience wasn't exactly the whirlwind of excitement they had anticipated, that they also felt homesick at times. By pretending that everything was 'fine' so that I wouldn't lose face, I think I lost an opportunity to connect with people around me on a deeper, and more genuine, level.

If I was talking to that 18-year-old today, I would give her a big hug. I'd tell her that she's not alone, that she's not strange. I'd tell her that there isn't anything wrong with her. I'd ask her to just be herself, to try to accept herself for who she is rather than for what she wants to be. I know that the person she wants to be is someone whom everyone will love because she feels that if everyone loves her then maybe that'll mean she's someone who is worth loving. If I could tell the 18-year-old me anything, I'd tell her that the most important thing is to learn to love herself. Only then will she be free.

Activity

Two things I will do to treat myself ...

This week:

This month:

This year:

The kindest thing anyone has ever done for me was ...

If I could give one piece of advice to a 13-year-old me, it would be ...

BALANCE

'Of course it's hard to break the circle. It's easier to hide away and pretend everything is fine. But if things are to get better then it has to be broken, and for me, the only way to snap that circle is to admit what's going on.'

Aisling O'Toole

Amy Colgan

You know that little bit of your brain that tells you that everything's probably going to be okay? There should be a name for it and a national holiday when we all celebrate it and sing songs about how great and wise it is.

See, that bit of my brain had always done its job pretty well, but I never really noticed or thought about how important it was. Everyone imagines the best and worst things that could happen in their lives – and certainly any kid that grows up watching Disney films, or *Indiana Jones* reruns, knows that fate is going to fling a few venomous snakes in your path, but you have a sense, deep down, that you'll be grand *really*, that you'll win the day, and even if you do find yourself sinking in quicksand there'll be a big stick to grab onto right before it swallows you up.

The summer after my graduation, after weeks of planning and plane tickets, excited phone calls and vaccinations, I went to India. It was going to be a big adventure, meeting my boyfriend who'd been there for the summer, and heading south to Kerala, to the Ganges in Varanasi and maybe even doing something deadly in Nepal. There might be Sherpas, or elephants, or dancing in a Bollywood film in Mumbai. Who knew, eh?

I was a little bit scared. I mean, it's hard not to be, what with all the good-natured advice you get before you go somewhere like India, from the multiple tropical diseases that you are almost definitely going to get, to how to get various insects out of your skin (shudder), to dear God, whatever you do, don't eat this and this, or this ... and someone always has a friend who got malaria or mugged or ended up in jail. I danced the line between being totally excited and totally freaked in the days before I left but, you know, ultimately, it would all be grand, right?

Well, this time it wasn't grand. From Kolkata airport to the full-on incredible shock to the senses that is India, the noise and the colour and the hot heady smells, it was mad and amazing and beautifully nuts – and I got sick. Properly sick. It was only the third day of the trip, and I ended up in a dusty hospital with a soaring temperature and no clue what was going on.

We missed our flight to Kerala as doctors looked puzzled and did more tests. Lots of people came to have a good look at me. They said I'd have to stay the night, and then another, and then another, as they tried to figure out what was going on. It really didn't seem plausible that I could've been so unlucky as to catch something serious in such a short time, but they couldn't rule anything out. The only thing we knew was that I wasn't getting any better. For the first time, the bit of my brain that told me things were going to be okay was silent. The result? I was really, really scared.

But after a week in the hospital, the highlights of which were an amazing curry, the glass bottles of Coca Cola we smuggled in, and the eagle that landed on my windowsill one evening, the mystery illness turned out to be an allergic reaction. Not good old India's fault after all, but unfortunately I wasn't fit enough for train journeys or Sherpas or Bollywood dancing, and the doctors in Dublin said I should come home.

It could have been so much worse. I was alive, for a start, and I was going to be completely healthy, so I was determined not to get all sorry for myself about it. From the little I knew about India, I knew there were people in the world who really understood what unfairness was, and having to come back to your lovely home and miss your fancy holiday didn't qualify me as being one of them. It was actually harder to deal with the guilt of scaring my family and friends half to death and causing such a fuss, and feeling like such a lame-ass for getting sick, but everyone was so kind and so frustrated on my behalf that this, too, passed before long.

I didn't realise it at the time, but what took longer to shake was the feeling that bad things could actually happen. I was scared that I would get sick in India, and I did, so who's to say the other things I worried about, the things everyone worries about, wouldn't happen too? If I had a headache, who's to say I wasn't going to keel over at any minute? I have this vivid memory of waking up one night with a pain in my chest and thinking, 'Ah right, it's all over, goodnight and good luck'. Sitting in lectures, dinners with friends – I'm pretty sure half the time I was quietly, almost unknowingly, certain that something bad was about to happen. It was like I had given that brilliant, brave bit of my brain (the bit that says it's all going to be okay) too much of a fright and now it was hiding in the dark.

It's not like I was jumping at my own reflection. I was getting on with things and I think I tried not to show how rattled I was. But people who knew me well definitely noticed. My mum, for one, and my GP for another. I think I went for a check-up for something – a headache or a stomach ache or something. My doctor must have guessed from the way I explained it that I was more worried than I should be, and she asked me why. I ended up telling her what had happened, and how shaken I was. She didn't seem the least bit surprised. She said that after a shock like I'd had, it was a pretty reasonable reaction. She said that she couldn't guarantee that I would never get really sick again, but that I wasn't really sick now, and if I ever was, she'd figure it out. She said that for all the bad things that can happen and the mad, bizarre or unlucky events that might strike, the belief that everything is probably going to be okay is almost always true. And that belief is far more helpful than its opposite.

A couple of years on, I've got it back – that little magic bit of my brain that reminds me that most things are okay, most of the time. Travelling the world, even the scariest parts of it, is one of the things that makes me happiest. And I guess if you asked me what I thought mental health was, that's it: the voice in your head that says, 'Hey, watch out for the quicksand, but if you fall in, there's bound to be a stick around here somewhere!'

Steve Wall

Over a number of years I've come to the realisation that it's good to scare the shit out of yourself every once in a while. To scare yourself so much that you wish you could run and hide. To put yourself in a situation where you have to summon all your inner strength to face your fears. But why the hell would anyone want to do that? Well, reader, let me share with you how I came to such a conclusion.

This realisation didn't present itself to me in any sort of revealing moment, like the answer to some nagging mystery. I just gradually copped on to the fact that anything good that has happened to me over the years has been a result of stepping outside my comfort zone and putting myself into a situation where I had to battle against my inner voices. I don't know what kind of inner voices you might have, but mine are usually critical and judgemental. Armed with chisels, their job is not to sculpt anything new but rather to chip away at something already created or to destroy a pure, new idea before it gets a chance to grow. Basically, nasty little bastards that live inside my head.

And then there's lying in bed. A bed can be a dangerous thing. Lying in your bed in the morning, staring at the ceiling and thinking about your life can be utterly detrimental to the day ahead, especially if you don't have warm company and it's even worse if you're hung-over. When you're in the supine position the inner voices always get the upper hand and you're easily overcome as if by an army of little people who have tied you to the bedpost and are hacking away at your dreams.

I never had any real game plan for my life, no goals and no vision of what might be possible. To me, life after the Leaving Cert looked like some sort of elongated summer holiday. After all, you're an institutionalised individual being cast, wide-eyed and clueless, into a deadly world. There was no such thing as career guidance in the school I attended and certainly no encouragement. The Christian Brothers just sent us off in a minibus to do exams for the banks and various semi-state bodies. Then I took the first college course offered to me: mechanical engineering. How I ended up doing that is beyond me. I hadn't even studied physics so it might as well have been Cantonese on the blackboard. I hated it and I was miserable. My classmates thought I was a prick as I skipped lectures and didn't hang out with them. I failed the first-year exams as I didn't even bother showing up. My parents were disappointed and I felt no one understood me. The truth is, I didn't understand myself.

Music was my first love, like it is for many people, but it wasn't exactly a career choice. I also loved films and reading plays and thought about maybe being an actor someday, but I had no idea how to pursue that from a small town in the west of Ireland in the depressed Eighties. This was a time before internet and even mobile phones, so when you were alone, you were ALONE. And you know what? I now realise that wasn't such a bad thing.

An American woman who had directed theatre in New York moved to the west of Ireland with her art-teacher husband

and decided to put on a play, Harold Pinter's *The Dumb Waiter*. I put myself forward for it and somehow got the part. It's a two-handed play and we rehearsed for a few weeks over the summer, just the three of us. The other actor was older than me and experienced. He was amazing and that just made me feel completely out of my depth. It was really intense as I'd never acted before and I was self-conscious even in rehearsals. I remember kicking myself for getting involved; it was hard work and the director was tough and drove me hard. There were days I felt like walking out and disappearing. 'Why did I get involved ... Aaaaagh ... I could be out having the craic with the lads and hitching around the county chasing girls and drink!'

Ah ... The drink. Yes, the drink also had a role. As you're probably aware, reader (and perhaps you have first-hand experience of it), the drinking in small-town Ireland is often on an epic scale not seen (or even understood) by the sensible urban dweller. As a teenager it was a badge of honour to have spent a night out with certain characters and tried to match them pint for pint until you had consumed your body weight in beer. I'm sure we've all witnessed individuals heaving up their stomachs in the toilets only to sit back down at the bar afterwards and order more. 'Sure, isn't he a mad bastard!' Looking back on nights like that I wonder (a) how I'm still alive and (b) why I thought so little of myself that I sunk to a level where I thought that was fun?

It was fear. And a fear of facing up to it. I had a vague notion of the person I wanted to be, but I didn't know who I was or whether I was actually any good at anything. My own judgement obviously couldn't be trusted as I'd already messed up with the whole college thing and now I found myself involved in this damned play, which had foisted great responsibility on me. People were relying on me. I was expected to show up, even though I was scared as hell and felt like doing a runner, but I couldn't. Everyone knows everyone in a small town and I wouldn't have gotten very far. Besides, everyone would know.

Like most lads growing up, I'd been in some hairy situations: motorcycle crashes, brushes with the law, fights in which I got beaten up and fights from which I came out alright … All the usual stuff. But the opening night of that play was easily the most frightening moment of my entire life. When the lights came up and I had to lower a newspaper to deliver my first line, I looked out and saw the silhouettes of the audience. That was one of those moments when you feel a tidal wave of pure fear rising up from your gut and you know that if you let it reach a certain point you are well and truly fucked (excuse my language but that's the only word that accurately describes the situation). I don't know how I managed to suppress that panic but I did and got through to the end of the play. Afterwards, I couldn't remember a single moment of the performance other than that initial battle with my inner demons, but I felt elated, like I'd grown a couple of inches or like I was floating on some sort of cloud. There were friends and family members in the audience and though they were there to lend me support, it can sometimes be harder to perform in front of people who know you so well. It can make it more difficult for you to escape from the image they have of you, from the person you are in their eyes. But escape I did – somehow.

Ever since the day I said yes to getting involved in that play I've managed to scare the shit out of myself regularly. Some years after that event I found myself in a rock band walking through a tunnel towards a huge stage to headline a music festival in Semple Stadium, Thurles, in front of over 40,000 people. Was I scared? I joked afterwards that I needed bicycle clips on my trousers.

Now I understand that fear is not a bad thing. It's there for a reason – to be faced up to. When the little people in your head brandish their chisels and try to chip a piece off the old block then it's time to go to war. They'll always be there, threatening to trip you up and making your life trickier. But it gives you something to push against, to overcome. It's what makes you YOU and it's what makes you unique. We all have our own inner battles and they form our character. That's what life is. It's not for thinking about; it's for living, for doing. Thinking about it too much is easy; it's the doing that's the hard part.

Now I think I need to scare myself again.

Sheila O'Flanagan

The *X Factor* of my teenage years was a show called *Opportunity Knocks*. Aspiring singers, dancers and musicians appeared on the programme in the hopes that they would be discovered and become a star. And, like *X Factor*, some of them did, although not all of them lasted the pace.

I remember watching it one evening and seeing a girl a few years younger than me winning the show. As I watched her being congratulated I couldn't help thinking that somehow I was already a failure. Here was someone who wasn't even in her teens and she was a winner on a television talent show. I couldn't keep a note in my head and had no chance of ever appearing on *Opportunity Knocks*. It seemed to me, at 15, that I was already a has-been, that I'd never be any good at anything.

I must have been going through a particularly bad period back then because I knew that I did have some talents, even if singing wasn't one of them. I was reasonably intelligent, I was doing well at school and I enjoyed writing for pleasure. Just because I couldn't sing didn't mean I was consigned to the scrapheap of life. It seems bizarre to me now that I was valuing myself against someone who had a talent I didn't, when I had different talents of my own.

Yet we all measure ourselves against other people, and it's easy to find ourselves wanting in some area. We think we're not as talented. Not as pretty. Not as clever. No good at sing-ing or dancing or ice-skating or football or maths or English or a million other things that the person we're comparing ourselves to at any particular moment excels in.

When society seems to place an extraordinary value on a skill we don't have (even if that 'skill' is just being famous for being famous), it's sometimes hard to remember the things we're good at ourselves.

Today, even more than forty odd years on, there are huge pressures on us to 'be someone'. Celebrity magazines and news programmes about the rich and famous rub our noses in the fact that we'll never have a ten-bedroom mansion in Beverly Hills or a yacht moored in Cannes. The lives of the super-rich have become normalised through the media, so that *not* living like Beyoncé or Kim Kardashian highlights our inadequacies.

But theirs are not normal lives. And fifteen minutes (or even slightly more) of fame does not make us good people, happy people or even successful people.

Success is all about learning from your mistakes, knowing that at the end of the day, you've made the most of what you have, and allowing yourself to be happy with your life.

As for the singer, I've no idea what she's doing with her life now, but I hope she's happy too.

Aisling O'Toole

It happened, as most things do, during an afternoon spent drinking. Now to clarify, I was on holidays and it was sunny. I wasn't just drinking gin from a hipflask at my desk – something I never do, despite the odd urge. However, despite the sun, the drinks and the lovely hotel, I was in desperate form and was brutal company, but as the drinks continued to flow and the beer garden started to empty, I started to talk.

And it was embarrassing. Unlike people I know who have real problems, I was just feeling a bit miserable. Things weren't falling into place according to the plan I set out when I was a teenager. Teenage me had believed that by the time I hit my early thirties I'd be editing a fabulous magazine, living with a dirty ride, thin finally, owner of a house filled with bunting and possibly thinking about babies. The reality wasn't quite measuring up and as I looked around and saw everyone I knew get married, celebrate promotions, have babies and buy houses while all I was buying was cheese and half-price bottles of wine, I felt absolutely shit about myself. If I'm being very honest, I felt jealous – incredibly jealous – of everyone.

Until I had it explained to me in a very slow, patient voice (by my very patient yet not-at-all slow friend), that comparison is ridiculous and jealousy pointless. Of course, with this realisation, we continued to plot until we had fixed all the problems of the world, the staff had closed the bar and we had all our clever thoughts written down on a receipt so we wouldn't forget them come morning. And the morning did come, bringing with it a banging headache and the realisation that we were not nearly as clever as we thought we were, but the insistence of my friend that comparing myself to others was making me miserable stayed with me, and has ever since.

It's not an easy thing to fix. I am a naturally jealous person and love when people are jealous of me (what's rare is wonderful, after all) so trying to look beyond the exterior circumstances of both myself and others is a constant struggle, and one I have failed at many times.

Before that cider-sodden afternoon, my jealousy had convinced me that all my friends liked each other more than me, to the point that I would stop all contact to see if they noticed. They did and – a word to the wise – people don't like it when their friends play games. Once was okay; by the fourth or fifth time their patience was wearing thin. So I'd retreat, disappear into a world of new people or new hobbies in an effort to try to prove I was as good as everyone else and then come back, but you can only break all ties and knot them back together again so many times before they need to be replaced.

Until another holiday afternoon, when everything finally made sense. A different hotel, the same wise and patient friend, and a rainy afternoon with only the bar for shelter. This time around we got straight down to business and within a few hours had come up with the theory that everything is a circle. And it is. Now we, of course, used this theory on everything from boys to food and the later it got, the more outlandish our claims became. In fact we even christened this circle The Daggerian Wheel, so convinced were we of its brilliance. But for me, it summed up exactly how I get caught up in cycles of melancholy. In fact, it's something I repeat to myself and others all the time. Part of the repetition is because it makes a lot of sense, the other part is hope that if I say it often enough it will sink deep into my brain.

Let me explain. As well as bouts of melancholy, I also have to be right. All the time. And I have to have the last word. All the time. Even with myself. So, if I'm feeling rubbish about work, instead of focusing on what's good elsewhere I'll look to everyone I know who's doing better than me professionally and, before I know it, I'm comparing my personal life to theirs and my financial situation to theirs, and whether it's what I want or not, I end up feeling like the world is against me. But that attitude does not a good friend make. In fact it makes me paranoid, paranoid to the point that I once took down all of my holiday photos because looking at them intently convinced me that Jane preferred Miriam and the photos made a mockery of me. (As an aside, I don't know a Jane, or a Miriam actually, but you get the gist.)

Anyway, back to the circle. So, paranoid and miserable, my friendships start to suffer and suddenly, without friends as a sounding board, I start picking fights with my family until I end up with nobody to talk to. When even your mammy has had enough, you have to admit things are bad. So at that stage, my days are pretty grim because I've pushed away everyone who entertains me and can only see badness. But see, I'm right after all: my world really is miserable. It just takes a while to see that I've made it as grey as it is.

Of course it's hard to break the circle. It's easier to hide away and pretend everything is fine. But if things are to get better, then it has to be broken, and I find that the only way to snap that circle is to admit what's going on. Sometimes even admitting it to myself, never mind somebody else, is struggle enough, especially when I hear tales of people going through real hardships, like illness, bereavement, bad haircuts or soggy chicken balls. Then I suddenly feel incredibly mortified at the things upsetting me. But I've learned the hard way that burying negativity only results in an eruption weeks later, usually over something trivial.

For me, it was all too often the misinterpretation of a text message ('You only used one exclamation mark instead of two; you're clearly still annoyed at me') or an overreaction to a well-meaning comment ('I am a grown woman and can wear a tracksuit every day if I want'). So instead of being embarrassed, I'm honest. I admit what's going on and I try to hang on to the friends I think have it so much better than me. Instead of comparing my real life to the fictitious one I've created for them, I sit and listen as they chat and bitch and laugh around me and try to remember that nobody has it easy, not even Kylie. And I struggled with that for a long time. I still do. But on my most recent holiday, when DVDs, magazines and a bottle of wine were the order of the day, I came across a quote from Theodore Roosevelt.

'Comparison is the thief of joy,' I said to my now slightly older and still wiser friend.

'You'd do well to remember that,' she said.

And I laughed. I laughed at what she had said and took it for what it was: a well-meaning comment.

A print of that quote now hangs in my house – well, my parents' house, which was defo not the plan at 33 years old – to remind me to always think of the bigger picture. And it does.

As for my teenage hopes, at least one of them came true. The rest will too, I hope – when and how they're supposed to.

Laura Whitmore

At 15, I thought I was a nerd. Fifteen was kind of horrible actually when I think about it. I was always the short one in class (something magically happened at 16 to make me the 5ft 8in I am today), and because I did well academically and was on the debating team, I certainly didn't consider myself cool. I had always enjoyed performing, but would find myself tongue-tied in certain situations. I remember a boy coming up to talk to me when I was in the Gaeltacht. My throat dried up, and I just didn't have a clue what to say back: what were you supposed to say to boys anyway?

A lot has happened since then, and I now earn my living by talking to people. I think the 15-year-old me would be pretty impressed – by my height if nothing else! My mum has always said that I was never cut out for a nine-to-five, conventional job, and I suppose I always knew that, too. She believed in me when I told her I was going to London, where I knew practically no one, to become a television presenter. I had to believe in myself that it would work out. Thankfully it did, and lots of other brilliant stuff happened too, so I'd like to think that my 15-year-old self would be proud of me for that.

Now, at 29, I'd love to tell the teenage me that life gets easier the older you get. Because it's true. The biggest thing I've found is that I care less and less about what other people think of me or what I do. That's something myself and my friends have been talking about a lot recently – how as you grow older you really do learn to accept yourself, rather than measuring your worth by others' opinions. I'm not saying that I woke up one day and suddenly decided to absolutely love myself, or feel amazing all the time, but I definitely like myself more, and it's time and experience that have made me feel comfortable in my own skin. I've also learnt that no matter what you look like, what your job is, or whatever, people are going to have opinions, good and bad. And I really believe you become stronger and happier as a person when you decide to go your own way.

Speaking of jobs, I'm not going to complain about mine. It's absolutely brilliant, and it takes me all around the world. I get to see amazing things and meet really interesting and talented people. But if there is a downside, it's that it can feel nonstop. I do feel stressed, sometimes, especially if I'm travelling a lot, and pressure comes with most of what I do. That pressure is necessary, as are the butterflies in my tummy before I do something scary, but the older I get the more I realise that I need other things in my life to balance that pressure out. The trouble is, when a day off does come around, I'm not the best at relaxing; I'm not very good at doing nothing! I feel like I should be busy all the time, that there's always more to do, and tend to feel guilty about just chilling out, but I'm working on that. I walk more, practise yoga when I can, and I've recently started taking 'Laura' days when it is just me, myself and I – being around people so much the rest of the time means I need that alone time, too.

My job might look scary, especially when it comes to presenting in front of a huge crowd or on live television. But you should know that I wasn't born ready to do this kind of thing – it has simply become easier by repetition; the more I've thrown myself into scary situations the more natural they have gradually begun to feel. I was talking to Ed Sheeran about this the other day. He was saying how he remembers first playing in front of 20 people, then 200, then 2,000, and then how he suddenly found himself in an arena performing for tens of thousands of people. I suppose it's worked the same way for me. Speaking on live television, or in front of a stadium of people, is petrifying when you think about it, but if you have plenty of practise under your belt you become increasingly confident that you can and will make the scary stuff work out. And you'll never know what you can achieve unless you push yourself into those frightening situations.

Do I have bad days at work? Yes. Nothing can go right all of the time, and when it has been a bit of a shitty day I know the best place to go: home to my couch. So it's straight back to my flat, comfy clothes on, friends around, curry in and as much Ben & Jerry's as we can handle. We watch box sets on Netflix, talk about stupid stuff, and make each other laugh. It works. The other option is to go out dancing. We don't have to go mental or anything, just find somewhere with good music and a dance floor that's ready for us. Dancing is something I've always loved to do, and I think it's pretty therapeutic, too.

Long-time friends are really important to me, and I'm lucky to have held on to some true friends from my primary-school days – one of my best friends lives with me now in London, and her friendship is a big plus in my life. I love that she knows me for who I am, not as the girl 'off the telly', and I know that I can talk to her if something – even if it's stupid – is bothering me. So that's one piece of advice I'd give: hold on to those old friends as tightly as you can.

It might sound cheesy, but there are a couple of little things I do to stay positive. I love a good inspiring quote, for one thing, and have been known to tweet my favourites. I love lines like, 'Stars can't shine without darkness', and am a big believer in what Dolly Parton says: 'You can't have a rainbow without a little rain.'

I suppose those kind of quotes are in line with my big motto in life: that everything happens for a reason. There have been times when I've found this really difficult to believe, times when something didn't go to plan either personally or professionally, but I always try to come back to the idea that everything works out as it is supposed to in the end. Maybe you can't understand why your relationship broke up, or why you didn't get a job you wanted, and it's hard to see how a negative thing could possibly become a positive. All I can say is that, in my experience, what seemed disappointing in the past has helped me to get to where I am today – including those jobs I didn't get, or the relationships that didn't, sadly, work out – and where I am today is happy.

There are loads more things I want to do, and more happy things I hope will come into my life. I hold onto these dreams by writing them down, and the blackboard in our flat is good for that. It's especially good when something goes wrong; we know it's time to pick up the chalk and write down a nice intention. Having these wishes on the wall is a reminder to make the good stuff happen, and ticking things off reminds me that it often does.

Apart from feeling more comfortable in my own skin, one of the biggest lessons I've learned recently is that nobody has a perfect life. I've made the mistake of believing a friend has everything sussed, that nothing could be going wrong in her world. But in time I've found that there is almost always something beneath the surface, and it's only in talking to people, and sharing your own stories, that you find this out. The person you think has everything worked out has worries, fears and disappointments, too – me included. So do talk, even when it's difficult. It will remind you that we're all in it together.

Activity

List three challenging situations in your life and
how you turned them into positives ...

Next time I feel out of balance I will ...

Call a friend

Watch an old movie

Write in a journal

Go for a run

Cook something nice

Pick your six favourite quotes from this book and write them here:

Display them somewhere you will see them every day.

REACH OUT

'With time I understood that I couldn't live
that way, so I took what initially felt like
a very difficult step – I asked for help.'

Brendan Courtney

Thomas Noonan-Ganley

My childhood was privileged – not so much financially
(although we never went short), but more so in terms of
the lifestyle and support we had. My parents are educated,
open-minded, caring and grounded. I also have three brothers I get on very well with, despite the occasional fights and
quarrels.

We'd lived in the UK and had experienced different cultures
and big-city life. Then, when I was 11, we moved to the west
of Ireland. My brothers and I thought of it as a big adventure:
swimming, roaming the lanes, building tree houses and sometimes being roped into helping with the gardens.

We were thrown into a whole new culture. Fascinating,
challenging and exciting, it was also hard work. Once
we'd settled in, as with most things, day-to-day life could
be mundane. It was also often grey and wet – it is Ireland
after all!

We lived in a potentially isolating part of the country, but had many friends. Some were 'local' Irish people and others were 'blow-ins' from all over the world. A good mix socially. Generally, these were very open, accepting and forward-thinking people. By chance we'd moved to an area that was quite culturally diverse.

School was school – but we got on with it. My ambitions for the future were high, and I had no problem announcing them to the world. I moved to Dublin to study, but a year later dropped out of college as the course wasn't for me. I thought I'd take time to figure out what I wanted. Working in retail and cafés, I also travelled a bit.

Ultimately I ended up living in Dublin, working in a job I didn't like, and living in a shared house with people I didn't feel comfortable with. I didn't know how on earth I'd ended up in this situation.

I felt stuck and wanted to move forward with my life, through study or career. But I didn't know what I wanted to do. On top of this I wanted liberty – to travel, see the world and never look back.

I was afraid that if I committed to study I would never be 'free'. But I was also afraid that if I just headed for the horizon then the opportunity to better myself would pass me by. As a result I did nothing. My life was frozen with indecision.

The road ahead seemed gloomy. I didn't know what to do or where to go. The same thoughts spiralled around my mind, often exhausting me. I just knew I didn't want to be living the life I was in.

To compound matters, I felt I shouldn't be in this situation. Surely with my upbringing, family, and the promise I'd shown growing up, I could do anything I wanted? There shouldn't be anything wrong with me. Those thoughts gripped me and kept me from truly addressing whatever I was going through. If people didn't look too closely, my life was fine. Feigning a cheerful disposition is not hard.

One friend, in whom I did confide, eventually encouraged me to see a therapist. She was undergoing regular counselling for her own issues and said she was worried about me. She'd asked her counsellor to recommend someone suitable. As I trusted her and didn't want her to worry about me, I arranged an appointment.

After the first session I decided to commit for a few months. I was lucky that my first therapist was suited to me, and I could work well with him.

I felt many things throughout my sessions – relief, anger, nostalgia, upset – but that, I learned, is the point. We all bob up and down emotionally throughout life. What's important is to know that these undulations are normal. We have to learn to accept our emotions, and not to let them run our life.

Therapy was hard work and change seemed to take a long time. But in the long term it has been extraordinarily successful. I went back to university and completed an honours degree. I'm working and now interning, and feel like I have options.

The most important changes to my life, however, are not so easy to measure in a tangible way. Knowing how to ground myself when I feel stressed or anxious and being able to break unhelpful thought patterns once I recognise them are two incredibly useful skills. Mindfulness in the everyday is something I try to work on.

I should note that I'm not always successful. I have bad days, harmful thoughts and sometimes I let my emotions get the better of me – but that's normal. As long as I keep working at being aware and grounded and I apply what I've learned through therapy, then I do okay.

I now view going to see a counsellor or therapist in the same way as I would view going to see a doctor. If you damaged your knee you'd see a professional, so why wouldn't you see a professional if you were struggling mentally or emotionally?

While I never thought there was anything wrong with the idea of therapy, I also never saw it as something for everyday troubles. I always thought therapy was for 'others', or for more 'serious' problems than mine. Well, that simply isn't true. Nowadays I tell anyone who'll listen that I've been to therapy, and that I still go if I feel the need. The idea of looking after your mental health should be normalised.

Although I hope never to end up as stuck and depressed as I was a few years ago, I'm also realistic. Things happen in life that upset your personal apple cart. The apple cart falling over is not the issue – knowing that it does sometimes fall over and learning how to prop it up again is.

Brendan Courtney

My name is Brendan, and – seeing as you're asking – here's my story. I have a great life, and I am happy. I love my jobs (I have a few!), love fashion, and love making exciting things happen. As a people person, I derive energy and happiness from big chats on all sorts of subjects with all sorts of people, and I think it's fair to say I am considered a fun and sociable person. My brain tends to work at a mile a minute, with ideas flying everywhere, and my mouth sometimes has difficulty keeping up with everything I want to say. My approach to life is based on believing in people's essential goodness, in karma, in family, and in working hard to turn dreams into realities. My outlook is so positive even *I* am jealous of me sometimes (I'm kidding ... kind of!).

But here's what you should know – I, like pretty much everyone I know, have had my adventures in mental health. Here's how they happened, and, most importantly, what they taught me about living.

The venue was the POD nightclub on Dublin's Harcourt Street, and I was 23. As a visual person, I often remember experiences by what I was wearing. On this occasion it was a Guardian Angels t-shirt, the kind worn by a crime-fighting group of New York's underground. I was there with my boyfriend of the time, and we were celebrating his birthday. It was a great, carefree night until something went very wrong. My boyfriend, it transpired, had stupidly taken five, or maybe six, ecstasy tablets. For the record I should say that I was not into drugs. I'm glad of that, because the next moment I looked around to see my boyfriend not smiling in front of me but motionless on the floor. He had collapsed. An ambulance was called. A visit to the accident and emergency room followed.

Things went downhill as he slipped into a coma. I remember standing there, terrified and helpless, faced with his impending death and knowing my Guardian Angels t-shirt wouldn't quite cut it. The good news is that he did regain consciousness, but he had come very close to losing his life, and something inside me shifted as a result. A normal night, a FUN night, had turned into something horrible, and that frightened me. The result? I suffered a severe panic attack.

So what exactly is a panic attack? It is an episode of paralysing fear brought on by anxiety, and – the doctors tell me – often linked to an underlying trauma or depression. It can manifest in many ways, but when it comes to a severe panic attack: trust me, you know *all* about it. My body had gone into an adrenaline shock. It felt like someone was running at me, wielding a knife. I was terrified, out of breath, and convinced I was having a heart attack. I tried to calm down, to control my breathing, but that made matters worse. My brain was fizzing over, causing confusion and terror. Simultaneously, I knew that nothing was happening to make me feel all of this. Put simply, I thought I'd lost it.

The attack eventually subsided, and I'm happy to report that I've never experienced anything of that level since. It soon became apparent, however, that I was going through life with the threat of a panic attack as my shadow.

That threat made me a more anxious, fearful person, and it placed question marks over my sense of self and strength of mind. With time I understood that I couldn't live that way, so I took what initially felt like a very difficult step – I asked for help.

I went to my GP, who referred me to an amazing therapist. She was so amazing that she was happy to take whatever money I had in return for her services. It could have been a fiver, or twenty quid: the thing is that she wanted to help me.

First, she told me that no one has ever died because of a panic attack. Then she told me to walk to the Hodges Figgis bookstore on Dawson Street. I was to look for the section on self-help and, specifically, on panic attacks. Instead of the single shelf I had expected, there was a whole wall of books on the subject. I thought: okay, that's reassuring; I'm clearly not the only person in this situation!

We then started cognitive behavioural therapy, which helped me get to grips with how I was feeling and to 'manage' myself when I began to feel in any way panicked. It made life ten times more bearable. On reflection, however, I'm not sure the issue was fully resolved.

Next came a new job. I had landed a role as a researcher and fashion reporter for RTÉ One's afternoon show, *Open House*. Under my remit was the 'Quacks & Whacks' section, meaning I would track down authors who had written books on new forms of self-help. I really went for it, but privately thought most of the subjects, like colour therapy, were a load of rubbish.

One day, however, a mind-blowing woman walked into the Green Room. Her name was Pauline McKinnon and she had written a book on something called 'stillness meditation'. Pauline had suffered with agoraphobia, finding herself scarcely capable of leaving her own home for eight years. Through extensive research she had discovered this new form of meditation, a precursor to today's uber-popular 'mindfulness'. I was fascinated. As a young person who did not believe in traditional religion, I had been looking for answers. I wanted to know why I was here, why things are so shit sometimes, and what's going on. Pauline's rationale was to use meditation to find those answers within.

Stillness meditation, or mindfulness, is like taking your brain out and rinsing it in lukewarm water before popping it back in. All your answers come out; your indecisions slowly but surely resolve themselves. Those hang-ups you consider so important? You realise they are petty and unworthy of your attention. The only thing wrong with meditation is that once you get your mind back in order you tend to stop practising and then you get stressed again ... So it's back in the room, and back to finding your centre again!

I digress. There I was in the Green Room, hanging on Pauline's every word. She put her hand on my shoulder and said: 'Something's really bothering you, isn't it?' I said yes and told her I had a severe panic attack and never got to the root of it. She looked me in the eye and told me I had to talk again, and I had to talk more this time.

Therapy round two! I went back to see someone, for ten weeks this time. We went deeper. We talked about the grief I experienced as a young child. Unfortunately, and very sadly, two sisters either side of me had died from congenital heart defects. One died when I was nine months old, another when I was 2 years old. I was so young you'd imagine I was unaware of what was going on, but of course I was aware – very aware of the trauma caused by two deaths in our family, the grief in our home – so I had developed this pathological fear of death. Then, when I became a young adult, and didn't believe in an afterlife, I had a freefall period; wondering where was I going and panicking about death. With therapy I conquered those fears and resolved my reasons for existing. I found happiness in simply being here.

As a television presenter I know you have to keep the script interesting. So, guess what? I later developed symptoms of obsessive-compulsive disorder! Great, right? Eh, no!

It happened at a really stressful time in my life. I had stopped meditating, had just bought a house; was shifting cities for a new job. I was tired, under pressure, and, to make matters even lovelier, I developed this obsessive fear of sharp objects. It sounds mental, doesn't it? I remember being in my apartment one day, looking at a knife on the counter. I thought to myself: I could pick that knife up right now and drive it into my heart. I was afraid of the knife, afraid of what I was capable of doing with it.

What a random, mad thought! But here's what I've learned: people have random, mad thoughts all the time, and being stressed can make these thoughts multiply. Then you think: 'I'm mad! What's wrong with me?!' It spirals out of control. When you are tired and stressed you grab that thought and run with it instead of saying: 'So what? It's just a thought ... Let it go.' Mindfulness teaches you to let it go. It teaches you that it is just a thought, not an action. I've since learned how to deal with having those funny thoughts, and how to make them melt away, but that's not to say the initial few months of OCD were easy. I thought I was a freak. I was mortified. And I didn't tell anyone about it.

I soon realised it was time for therapy round three. Just six weeks this time, and a course of cognitive behavioural therapy with a strong emphasis on relaxation techniques. And yep, you guessed it, it worked.

As you may have worked out by now, I'm all for therapy. In fact, if ever I make enough money I'm going to gift a ten-week therapy course to each of my friends! And I'm all for meditation – I'll stick on a meditation session when on a plane, and go to the Oscailt Centre on Dublin's Pembroke Road every year for their six-week mindfulness course.

We all go through periods of doubt and anxiety in our lives, and many of us question what the point of it all is. Through therapy and meditation I've found that I have lots of questions, and that's okay. I won't get all the answers: that's the beauty of life. I've also adopted the concept of karma, and now live my life truly believing that what you give out you get back. It could be as simple as how you walk into a room. Walk in with your head down and chances are no one will speak to you, and you'll leave unhappy. Walk in with fun and friendliness and you could leave the room with a new job. It can be hard at times, I know (you wouldn't like me when I'm grumpy...) but if you can try to practise positivity I promise it will improve your life. If nothing else, being nice to people will make *you* feel better: think of it as selfish if you like!

For me the point of life is other people, and living on through the little people coming into the world. I'm not sure if I will ever become a parent, but for now I am happy to help parents in my world however I can, whether that's through having a laugh, being a distraction, babysitting or whatever. I think the homosexual leg of any society is really important, actually, when it comes to providing that supportive role for families and parents.

However your life develops, I urge you to live it as fully as you can. Be grateful for when and where you were born – this is an Irish generation with limitless possibilities. Think about this luck, and remember that throughout your life luck will be a combination of preparation and timing. So if you want something, do the homework, then grab that opportunity when it arises.

If you're the kind of person who has a very fast-moving mind, like I have, or if you're the kind of person who can easily slip into negative thought patterns, you really need to learn how to understand that. The good news is that with a bit of training – whether it's CBT (Cognitive Behavioural Therapy) or whatever – you'll find that you can actually control these things quite easily, if you're anything like me. And another thing I should tell you: when you learn how to control your own mind, to keep it healthy, you become one hundred times more powerful than you could have imagined before.

Life for me today is about enjoying, and taking note of, the simple things. I look at the love around me, and am grateful for it on a daily basis. And here's the thing: I'm not sure I could say that if it hadn't been for my 'adventures' in mental health. Tough times have made me a happier, healthier person, and someone who is always ready for the next adventure.

Rosemary McCabe

When I was 8 years old, a friend of mine died in tragic circumstances. At the time, I thought of her as my best friend, although now I'm not so sure – when you're 8, you have a different best friend each day. Still, we were close. A week previously, we had celebrated her birthday in McDonald's in Bray. I remembered piling into the car to go home, our sandals full of sand and the floor of the car overflowing with shells.

When I was 19, I broke up with my first boyfriend. We had been dating for three years; he was my everything, and I his, but the intensity made living life – the days we were apart, the times we spent with friends and family – difficult. When I decided to go 'down the country' to university, he offered to go with me, to live with me, to wait at home for me every day while I went about my new life. That we broke up wasn't a huge surprise, but the aftershocks were, for me, unexpected. I felt bereft in a way I hadn't known possible; I expected him to arrive at my door, in my shared dorms, any day. I saw him around every corner – although mostly, I suppose, because I wanted to. He never came.

When I was 21, I found myself spearheading a sort of revolution in a college society of which I was a member. We disagreed with the actions of our chairperson – he had become, we thought, drunk on power and we wanted him ousted or, at the very least, alerted to his dictator-like tendencies. My coup was a monumental disaster. Despite the support of what felt like a majority, there were three or four of us who were pushed out of the group. The society stood by its leader, and abandoned us; I felt the loss of those who had been close friends keenly. I had never felt quite as alone as I did in those few weeks – nor have I experienced such feelings of isolation since.

These are all very simple, basic, *human* examples of shit things that happen along the way in most people's lives. We lose friends, one way or another. We experience bereavement, and the dissolution of relationships, and we fall out with people.

When I began experiencing feelings of depression – in my case, a profound sadness that descended upon me when I awoke and left only when I slept (which, thankfully, and unlike many people, I continued to do) – I looked to each and every one of these events to find an excuse, a reason, for how I was feeling.

Maybe I hadn't dealt with the death of my friend; at the time, the early 1990s, schools weren't as in touch with the theories of psychology and psychiatry as they are now. We received no counselling. Instead, we lit candles and held hands and shared our stories, but we were expected, by and large, to get over it eventually.

Perhaps it was that first, traumatic breakup. Maybe we were meant to be together; soon after our parting, he moved abroad – this man who had, until then, seemed content to live in the same small town living the same small life forever – and I felt even further betrayed by this giant leap he had taken. I imagined myself the more adventurous of us two, but now he had left me, good and proper.

Or was it the feelings of isolation that came with this large group falling-out I had in my college years? Did I feel in some way undervalued, unloved, worthless, as a result of being cast aside by my peers?

I went to see a counsellor, first in university, who advised me to imagine my problems as being encircled in a large balloon. She asked me to hold the balloon in front of my body, to pass it along – to her, or to anyone, as a way of getting rid of it. My scepticism won out and, after the balloon episode, I didn't go back.

I went, again, to speak to a counsellor a few years later, while I was completing a master's in journalism. I still felt sad, without reason and with little relief. He talked kindly to me about my perceived 'problems' but never, I felt, got to the root of anything. (I never really felt I could bring up my friend who had died, or my school boyfriend – the former felt as if I would be cashing in on someone else's tragedy, the latter as if I were auditioning for a part in a high-school musical.)

After about four years of feeling pretty rubbish, off and on, I went to my doctor. Going to the doctor seemed like a last resort, like what you did when you had accepted that you couldn't talk your way out of your problems, what you did when you were ready to be medicated.

She advised me to speak to another therapist, which I did. We mostly focused on the fact that I was feeling distant from my school friends, from my sister, from my parents. I felt detached, somehow, as if I were leading a different life, on a different path, to everyone else.

It was my sister who urged me, finally, to go back to my doctor. The therapy, though I enjoyed talking about myself, uninterrupted, for an hour a week, wasn't achieving much (although my last therapist did advise me to try mindfulness meditation, which I did, and find very helpful for clearing, if not curing, the mind).

'They've developed medication to fix things,' she said, over email, from New York. It's not a coincidence, I don't think, that my US-dwelling sister is the only person I know aside from my doctor who is not anti-medication. 'I know loads of people who are on medication for depression and anxiety – some for a short time, some for a longer time. It could help you get back on track.'

So I went back to my GP and told her that the therapy wasn't working in my opinion.

'I think I'm ready to try medication,' I said.

'I think you're right,' she said. 'Sometimes the chemicals in our brains get a little mixed up, and all we need is a little kick-start to get them right again.'

In all, I was on medication (an SSRI, selective serotonin reuptake inhibitor) for a year. In that year I felt worse and then, slowly but surely, I felt better. I stopped feeling isolated from my loved ones. I stopped being afraid to socialise in large groups. I stopped hating myself and everyone else. I stopped waking up and feeling sad, and going to bed and feeling sad. And then, I stopped taking my medication (under the supervision of my doctor). And I waited to feel worse.

But I didn't. Sure, I had moments where I felt a bit rubbish. But, crucially, I had moments where I felt wonderful. When Germany beat Brazil 7-1 in the World Cup semi-finals, for example, I felt a bit sad for the Brazilians. When I found myself, with four hours' sleep, in a Spanish airport gazing at a 'flight cancelled' board, I felt livid. When I saw the first picture of my new nephew, I felt overjoyed.

Now, I sometimes panic when I feel sad – terrified that I'm getting sick again. Then I remember that feeling sad is okay when it's not every day; I enjoy feeling the full spectrum of emotions, from sad to happy, angry to frustrated, envious to accepting.

I do yoga sometimes. I meditate when I remember. I take a lot of deep breaths and count to ten when I feel myself descending into panic (usually facing into a very busy week with very little visible open space in my organiser).

What's most important, I think, is that I give myself a break. When I quit my job I felt super anxious – and I let myself. Changing jobs is stressful, and I'm only human. When I almost missed a recent flight to Dallas and thought my heart would leap out of my chest as I queued at American immigration,

I tried to feel it all – the fear, the anxiety, the nerves – and then let it go.

I made it in the end – through the sadness and, almost as importantly, through the immigration queue.

Activity

Find a photo of someone or something you can always rely on to make you smile and stick it here ...

(It can be a person, a pet or even a plant!)

Who is the first person I would talk to if I was feeling ...

Happy

Stressed

Sad

Excited

Scared

Proud

CREATE

'Some people find God,
some find exercise –
I found writing.'

Emma Hannigan

June Devaney

When I first discovered I was pregnant I didn't know what I would do. I was still in school. My parents had recently separated. I had left home with my mum and the love of my life was threatening to leave me if I didn't terminate the pregnancy.

After many heart-wrenching conversations and arguments, I decided a termination was not what I wanted to do, so I was left alone to face the pregnancy and the prospect of being a teenage parent. I spent a lot of time in denial, but it soon turned to panic as I realised the time would eventually come for me to break the news to family and friends.

At seven weeks, I met with a crisis pregnancy counsellor through my GP. It felt better to finally tell somebody about the worries and fears I had about pregnancy, birth, my future and telling my family. It was a relief to know I was not completely alone as I faced them. It was also the first time I could speak to someone about the heartbreak I was feeling about my relationship ending.

After ten weeks I told my mother, whose reaction was much better than anticipated. Of course she was disappointed, angry and heartbroken but she swore she would support me in whatever I decided to do.

Telling peers and teachers was a real test. Every day I faced whispering in the corridors, heads turning to stare at me in the canteen and sometimes even blatant disregard from teachers and people I once considered to be my friends.

It was very difficult to ignore it all. I struggled regularly with the decision to leave school or to stay and plough through. But I knew I would need my education for both our futures

I kept in contact with my crisis pregnancy counsellor, who supported me in making plans for labour, the hospital stay and life after the baby came. I also confided in my GP regularly about any other concerns I had relating to my changing body and the different feelings and emotions that came with pregnancy.

In the summer before my Leaving Cert I had a healthy baby boy. It was only eleven days after my eighteenth birthday and although I was now legally deemed an 'adult', on the inside I felt like a scared child, holding onto my mother and never wanting her to leave my side. The future terrified me. 'How would I get through this?' I would think, and 'How far would my savings get us and how long would they last?'

School was restarting in September, and with it came thoughts like, 'How would I make it through the Leaving Cert?' Other people even placed bets on how long it would be before I dropped out. And what about my dreams of college and a career? What kind of life could I provide if these people were right?

I returned to school in September regardless. I was determined to complete the year and continue to college to pursue a career in midwifery. I stayed up all night, every night, with a crying newborn and still buttoned up my school shirt every morning to be in class for 9 a.m. My mother, my rock, helped immensely when she offered to mind him during the school day and sometimes she would help in the evenings to let me study as it grew closer to exam time.

The lack of sleep and little time to properly care for myself quickly became physically and emotionally exhausting. I soon found myself crying along with him during the night. I ploughed on, however, always trying to keep a brave face and refusing to admit that I was finding things difficult.

At one point the public health nurse, who visits after a baby is born, noticed my change in mood and suggested I speak to the GP about possible postnatal depression. I was too tired and agitated to take her seriously. Besides, I had read stories in magazines about women with postnatal depression and I believed my bouts of crying were nothing in comparison to what I had read.

After sitting my exams twice, I received an offer for the university course I wanted in Galway. However, childcare costs meant I couldn't take my son with me for the first few months. It was extremely difficult to leave him, but my mother assured me that he would be okay with her and that he needed me to do this, for both our futures.

Every Sunday, I cried on the bus the whole way to that empty apartment in Galway. And even though I knew this college opportunity was what I had worked so hard for, the guilt I felt after leaving him was unbearable.

I threw myself into my studies and rarely lifted my head to take part in the activities and social life around me. My friends eventually stopped inviting me to events and began to move on with their lives. Seeing photos of them on Facebook, enjoying college life or travelling abroad for their gap year, I felt left behind and very lonely.

I soon became angry at the world because I wasn't living the life I had planned. I was angry at my friends for leaving me behind, I was angry at my ex for walking away and not sharing responsibilities, I was angry at the system for not supporting a mother to afford childcare while in education and I was angry at myself for not being at home to look after my son.

I soon began to berate myself for the smallest things and then would eat and eat in an attempt to comfort myself. Soon my body began to react to the abuse I was giving it by eating junk food and abandoning physical exercise. I never had energy and constantly felt lethargic and tired. I was getting two to three hours sleep each night, which affected my concentration and thinking, which in turn affected my studies, which in turn accelerated my guilt about being away from home, which in turn became a bout of comfort eating. I was trapped in a vicious circle.

It wasn't uncommon for me to struggle to get up in the mornings but when that struggle turned into sheer dread of waking up at all, I knew I had to do something about it.

I suddenly remembered what the health nurse had said to me in the earlier days about postnatal depression and then remembered how good it had felt to confide in the GP and counsellor during my pregnancy. So I made an appointment to see my GP again and in the meantime I popped into a service near my apartment which specialises in youth health.

I wasn't sure what I wanted from the service when I first went in and I thought they would think I was crazy for just showing up out of the blue, but I was pleasantly surprised. I was met by a woman who made us both a cup of tea and sat down to have a casual chat with me about everything ranging from the weather to college to *Grey's Anatomy*.

She recognised, even from our short conversation, that I was in quite a vulnerable position and assured me that I could call in any time for support, advice or even just company.

I took the plunge and used the service a few times during the time I was there. Letting my guard down and trusting someone with the things I was struggling with was daunting at first but it was one of the best decisions I've ever made. Having my feelings validated helped me to understand that it's okay to not be okay sometimes, especially when things seem insurmountable.

I spoke to my GP at home also who echoed the nurse's opinion that my experience of pregnancy and the stress of life after the birth probably led to some postnatal depression and anxiety, and dismissed the common myths associated with postnatal depression that I had read about in magazines.

Over time I worked through a lot of issues, falling down and getting back up, falling down again and getting back up again. My support worker caught me with each fall but she wasn't the person to pick me back up. Instead she supported me in figuring out how to get up by myself and keep my balance. It is something I will never forget how to do now.

There was no miracle solution behind the doors of that service. It was simply a space where I had support in learning how to help myself. I realised that the key to my well-being and ability to get through tough times was already within me. I just needed to learn how to access it and to use it.

Now, when faced with seemingly insurmountable challenges, I have to remember to tap into my innate coping skills and remind myself that I have the strength, I have the courage, I have the potential, I have the intelligence to get through, just like all the other tough times I've managed to get through.

After I left Galway, I set up my own mental health campaign called 'Mind Your Mind' and spent my gap year speaking in schools, at conferences and on television about the importance of looking after one's mental well-being. I've also become a peer educator on a sexual health education programme for secondary schools and the crisis pregnancy counsellor I met during my pregnancy is now one of my supervisors on the programme.

Soon I will be starting my new part-time job as a support worker while finishing my degree course in college. My little boy started 'big school' this year, which he is very excited about.

The darker days are non-existent now, but there are still days when I'm stressed about exams, run down physically or perhaps a little upset or anxious about various things, but my coping techniques are never too far from mind. These might just help you too.

Alone time

It's very important for me to make time to be alone every day, even if it's just for five minutes. I sit somewhere quiet just to take a breath, give myself some space and recharge myself before re-entering a group. Even if I am at a party or a lecture; if I feel overwhelmed, I find it useful to take a walk to the bathroom for a few minutes to de-stress.

Exams

My approach to exams has changed dramatically. Instead of spending the last hour before the exam cramming in the last few bits, I use that hour to relax, meditate, listen to music or eat. I find I perform much better if I take an hour to 'chill out' before heading to the exam hall.

Knowing triggers

I've learned what triggers make me anxious or frustrated. Instead of feeling like I need to eliminate these from my life, which can sometimes be impossible, I have learned to recognise the trigger, to know the feeling and to sit with it until it passes. Sometimes, if I feel overwhelmed, I tap my foot on the floor to 'ground' myself and recognise that my thoughts need to be on the present moment and not on the trigger.

Knowing when to reach out

Still, there are times when I struggle to get through particularly tough times or when I'm faced with a situation where I don't know what to do.

Sometimes I look online for advice. Websites like ReachOut. com have lots of helpful advice or stories from other people, which I often take advice from when dealing with difficult situations. It is also very reassuring to know my GP is there for me, if I ever need her for serious concerns.

Oliver Clare

It was nearing 6 a.m. as I zigzagged along a narrow, winding road through the heather-covered mountains and picturesque lakes of Connemara, wearing nothing more than a pair of GAA shorts and a red sports singlet. My Garmin running watch wasn't built to hold a charge for any longer than seven hours, so I had it hooked up to a portable battery in a pouch around my waist, the wires taped up my arm with Velcro. It was a slapdash setup, but I was approaching the twenty-four-hour mark and wanted to keep a data log as a memento. Over the previous night, I'd horsed through a fierce amount of Jaffa Cakes, Kit Kat bars, chocolate muffins, Muller rice, a dozen bottles of Lucozade Sport and various other oddments.

This was my fourteenth marathon event of the year, and my first Ultra Marathon. At this point in the race, my body had already crashed three times: the first instance took place after I'd reached the 26-mile mark (when I'd normally be finishing up) and I had to force myself to continue running. About 40 miles later, I had made a stop at the Lough Inagh Lodge Hotel and tried to squeeze in a half hour's sleep. By now, my body was experiencing all manner of lovely side effects, the least charming of which were the violent spikes in body temperature. I spent most of that pit stop lying on a couch in the hotel drawing room, staring at the ceiling and trying not to throw up on the floor.

The final big crash occurred around the 70-mile mark, when I jumped into my support crew's jeep to grab a quick muffin. I didn't have any compression gear or extra layers on, and when I hopped back out of the jeep, the night wind hit me like a train. I ran perhaps four steps before every nerve lit up inside me, and I just screamed and screamed.

Right then, I wanted nothing more than to stop. And to sleep.

The problem was, we were working within a strict time limit. If I didn't cross the finish line by the thirty-hour mark, I'd be disqualified and wouldn't be allowed to finish. Proceeding ahead of me in the jeep, my support crew were told that we had miscalculated the remaining distance to be covered, and if we were to pull this thing off, I wouldn't be able to rest again and would even need to speed up.

Daybreak was approaching, and my body felt worn to shreds, but the dawn air was salty and refreshing. Despite the pain in my bruised and blistered feet, I attempted to tune out and enjoy the scenery. I had seen every inch of Connemara along the routes of two previous regular-length marathons, but this was different. As the roads were deserted, everything around me felt very serene and calm, much quieter than usual. The first light of the new morning seemed to revitalise me. Or perhaps it was just the Jaffa Cakes.

Back in December 2011, when I first came up with a mad plan to run twenty Irish marathons, I received a number of responses, most of which shared a common theme: 'Have you any idea what you've let yourself in for, Oliver?' 'Nice knowing you, Ollie!' 'Ehh, good luck? Madman ...' One minute I was at my desk, doing bank reconciliations and journal listings in my sensible Thursday office wear, the next I was sitting in a café across from Nigel and Vince from ReachOut. com, sketching out the beginnings of a strategy for a fund-raising and awareness campaign that would consume my life for the next twelve months.

The following March, I stepped out onto the road for my first official race and the mission was underway. It all started with a half-marathon in an idyllic country parish in the middle of Meath.

The morning started off warm and clear as the runners milled around excitedly. The name of the parish was Bohermeen, a corruption of an ancient Irish name, *An Bóthar Mín*, which means 'the smooth road', but there was nothing smooth about the road ahead. I remember getting a slagging from some of my fellow Drogheda AC runners for showing up in a beanie hat and long-sleeved cotton jersey – but after barely an hour of running, hailstones began to bucket down from the sky. Inclement weather would become a recurring theme of the blog I set up at runningforreachout.ie.

Alongside me on many of my trips around the country would be Frank McDermott from the Marathon Club of Ireland, who has since established the East of Ireland Series of marathons, which take place mainly around the Dublin/Meath area. He and the other members of the MCI family were always an invaluable source of advice ('Don't start off too quickly, keep your heart rate below 160 BPM for the first 13 miles and leave something in the tank for the end.' 'Don't wear a new pair of runners on a race day – get them worn in first.' 'Don't be afraid to take your walking breaks when you need them ...') as well as banter. And, as many people seemed to see me as some sort of crazy masochist, sometimes it was just nice to be around folks who didn't regard running weekly marathons as an unusual pursuit!

That summer had been a frenetic whirlwind of activity: a mad scramble of 4 a.m. starts, cross-country drives, training, blogging, interviews and fundraising events. I ran every kind of marathon imaginable – on roads, on mountains, in a forest, doing loops on a track, indoors, back-to-back, three in three days, another at midnight – basically anything I could think of. Being a year-long campaign, there were both high and low points, and when August rolled around, we were in the middle of a very low ebb; I hadn't raced in a few weeks and donations had slowed down to a trickle.

So, pretty much on a whim, I decided that in order to breathe some life back into the campaign, something monumentally crazy would be required. At one of the marathon club's early-morning B&B get-togethers, before a marathon in Dervock (Northern Ireland), I floated my new plan to my fellow runners around the breakfast table.

The responses were unanimous. 'Don't even think about it,' said one of the guys. 'Sure that's nearly four marathons back-to-back.' An experienced ultra runner chimed in from the other end of the room: 'That's right. If you're interested in doing ultra marathons, you'd want to start slowly. Do a 50k and build up to 50-milers or maybe a 100k.' All good advice, but deep down I knew I'd already made up my mind to run the Connemara 100 Mile Ultra Marathon, the longest single road race in the country.

I was in no way equipped to make the jump to an ultra. I definitely hadn't been training with anything longer than a standard 26.2 miler in mind. If anything, I'd been easing off on the training as the year wore on. But by the following week, the race director Ray O'Connor gave me the go-ahead and three days before the race I had my support crew in place. The team consisted of my dad, my aunt Rosaleen, and a great physiotherapist from Ballsgrove by the name of Brian Milne.

After a runners' meeting the night before the race, Ray pulled me aside.

'This is unlike anything you've ever done before and there are a lot of things that could potentially happen,' he explained. 'You could get sick, start hallucinating and talking gibberish or you could start making bad decisions as the race wears on. You've got to allow yourself to rely on your support crew; that's what they're there for.'

I nodded along, hoping not to give any hint of how truly unprepared I was feeling for the task ahead. 'I'm happy with the game plan you've laid out,' Ray told me. 'And I've no doubt you can finish this.' After hearing about everything that could go wrong, I wasn't so sure ...

Suddenly it was happening. Although my conversation with Ray had taken place just over a day before, it felt like a dream from way back in the past. The course is shaped like a giant figure of eight, with the 10-mile-long Inagh Valley running smack dab through the middle. For most of the day, I had been getting texts from friends and messages of encouragement on social media. By the time I made my way out of the valley for the second time, and began to head west towards the village of Roundstone, most of them were long asleep.

Known for its fishing and its traditional arts and crafts, Roundstone isn't exactly what you'd call a teeming hive of activity. We were warned ahead of time, however, that people were known to stagger out of the pubs after last orders and harass the runners. After spending over 80 miles on my feet, I was in no mood to deal with outside interference, but thankfully that never came to pass.

At this point, I was too tired to hold anything for myself. Rosaleen started running alongside me, a bottle of Lucozade mixed with dissolved salt tablets in her right hand, a flask of protein shake in the left. I ditched the tracksuit and my soaking wet poncho – losing the weight of all that extra gear was a godsend. However, at that moment, the aforementioned disaster appeared to strike, as we realised we had miscalculated the route and one of the stewards told us we were 7 miles further from the finish line than we had thought. Although I had slowed down considerably during the night, I kept moving forward and the psychological boost I got from crossing the 90-mile mark kept me going. The remainder of the course was littered with little hills, but as Rosaleen said, 'They're annoying wee f***ers, but they're doable!'

Because of the way the course is measured out, the race rather cruelly required runners to reach Clifden, where the finish line is, then complete three more laps of the town before being allowed to actually cross it.

Finally, with the help of another runner, Thomas Bubendorfer, I crossed the line to plenty of applause and back-patting, comfortably over an hour under the cut-off point, before promptly collapsing in a heap on the footpath. Twenty-eight hours, forty-seven minutes and forty-three seconds after the race began, it was all over.

Finishing that race seemed to have accomplished exactly what I had hoped for; the 'Running for Reach Out' campaign received increased newspaper and social media attention in the weeks and months that followed, and as a result, we did eventually hit our target of €5,000 in sponsorship.

This leads me to one final point. The following week, when I was back in Drogheda and hobbling my way around the running track, Barney Flannery (one of our group coaches) asked me why I'd want to do such a thing to myself. It's an excellent question, and one I had been studiously dodging all year because I just didn't want to talk about it. The truthful answer would simply be this ...

A while back, I lost a good friend to suicide. Sometimes I think back on the things I said or occasionally blogged about during that time and there is a palpable sense of guilt threading through most of it. In the logical part of my brain, I don't think I really believed that I was directly to blame in any sense, or that I could have changed that outcome. But still, I had an overwhelmingly strong feeling that I could have done something differently – anything, really – I could have been that little bit more perceptive, been a better friend, been there when it mattered most. The 'Running for Reach Out' project began, I suppose, as a way to try to honour my friend's memory, perhaps as a way to atone for this self-perceived failure, but also as a way for me to work through those feelings and to help myself through the grieving process. I wanted to support an organisation that was doing something positive in the field of mental health.

ReachOut.com turned out to be the perfect choice because of the nature of their services, their philosophy that 'everybody knows somebody going through a tough time', and their emphasis on youth and peer support. Because of the support I received from Nigel, Elaine, Roisin and the rest of the gang in the Reach Out offices, the project eventually grew into something very special, and it turned out to be a very positive year in my life. I owe them an immense debt of gratitude for that.

To anybody reading this, I'd only ask that you support Reach Out Ireland and groups like them whenever you can. They do such great work in providing support to those who need it and we should definitely support them in turn. To people who are going through a tough time, and those who love them, all I'd say is to remember that you're not alone in what you're going through, and that help is always there. The scariest moment is always just before you start learning to accept and deal with these sorts of feelings. After that, things can only get better.

Emma Hannigan

The importance of our mental well-being cannot be stressed enough. During our lives many of us battle illness at some point. In my case the sickness I happen to grapple with is cancer. Obviously this is a physical illness but, believe me, all the mind stuff comes into play too.

In my case cancer came with a precursor in the form of the cancer-carrying gene *BRCA1*. When I was diagnosed as a carrier I knew I had an 85 per cent chance of developing breast cancer and a 50 per cent chance of developing ovarian cancer. I had a choice. I could sit and wait for cancer to strike or opt for preventative surgery. In 2006 I had a bilateral mastectomy and my ovaries removed. Problem solved, right?

I thought so too. But life has a way of throwing curveballs and I happened to catch one. In 2007 I was diagnosed with cancer for the first time. Cue the piano falling out of the sky.

This wasn't meant to happen. I did all the right things. I tried my best, yet cancer still had the cheek to attack. Even though this most certainly wasn't on my wish list and it couldn't have been less welcome, I knew I still had a choice. I could decide how I was going to deal with it mentally.

Should I lay down and admit defeat or should I learn to play that imaginary piano that had descended from above at a rate of knots?

I realised that there was no reason why I should let the cancer win. I believed the physical part would be sorted by the doctors. I am incredibly fortunate to have an amazing team of oncologists and nurses who mind me and afford me the very latest intelligence and medications. So I knew I could concentrate on the mental stuff.

In short, I knew I needed to write a new tune on this offending piano and learn to dance to it.

After many relentless hours in a hospital bed, I came to terms with my cancer diagnosis and realised I still had power. I could still control what went on in my own head.

I knew I needed an outlet. The thoughts that zoomed around my head needed to get out. I talk *lots*. Ask my husband and children – I never stop! But the calibre of talking that's required when something is going drastically wrong is quite different.

I'm lucky to have amazing family and friends who would literally do a Bruno Mars for me and catch that proverbial grenade. But I knew this cancer backlash required another level of spleen venting.

Some people find God, some find exercise – I found writing. At first I simply logged what was happening in a matter-of-fact manner. Then I padded it out and wrote how it all made me feel. It was cathartic and freeing in a way I'd never thought possible. Once I began writing, it was as if this wonderful being that had been lying dormant inside of me had been unleashed. I turned those initial ramblings into a novel and miraculously in 2009 my first book, *Designer Genes*, hit the shelves.

During the years that followed my books have kept me sane. To date I've written six novels and my memoir detailing my cancer battle called *Talk to the Headscarf*. There is nothing like writing for me. I can escape to another world where none of the pressures of being a mum, wife, daughter, friend or family member exists. All that I see and hear are the voices of my characters and the places they inhabit.

I still talk all the time too. I do that on television, radio and in print. I regularly discuss cancer and the knock-on effect it can have on people's lives in the hope that it will all become less of a taboo.

Each time I talk, I learn more. Why? Because when I share part of my story, people do the very same thing right back. Talking opens doors. Talking honestly shows others that we don't need to feel alone. There is always someone out there who understands.

I can't choose whether or not I get cancer again. I am well aware that cancer doesn't care about me or anyone else it preys upon. No illness does. So I've always been of the opinion that I shouldn't show it any respect. Instead I choose to stand up and punch back with positivity.

If I wake up feeling low, I force my body into the shower and I go through the motions of getting dressed, doing my hair and putting on my makeup. By the time I'm on the school run with my children or in my office I'm in the zone. I'm ready to face the world. Even if I'm having treatment and feeling physically exhausted and need to go to bed that afternoon, I know I've embraced the day and taken part in what the world has to offer.

I know that isolating myself and shying away from day-to-day living doesn't help. I have always been a glass-half-full type of person and being sick hasn't quashed that. Sickness doesn't define me. I am not cancer. I am still me.

I don't look back in anger and I never question why I've been sick so often. To date I've had cancer nine times.

For me, acceptance affords peace of mind. After all, why would I battle against an illness only to spend my life lamenting? Instead I intend living each day to the full, enjoying my family and friends, doing the very best I can in work and play. Life is very precious. It's up to each one of us to make the most of it. Nobody else can make you happy. It starts from within. There is so much to see and do in this world. Grab the good times and endure the bad. The grass isn't greener on the other side.

Everybody is battling something in their lives. But that doesn't mean every day needs to be shrouded in darkness. Reach out to others. Talk, share and be there.

We can't stop those pianos from falling out of the sky, but we can try our best to learn to play a happy tune.

Wishing you all love and light and many precious days of happiness!

'Life is not about waiting for the storm to pass, It's about learning to dance in the rain.'

Vivian Greene

Activity

Describe an experience in your life when you surprised yourself with your own abilities ...

Take a creative challenge: take a photo every day for the next week ...

Day 1: Something that makes you smile

Day 2: Something or someone that inspires you

Day 3: Something that you're thankful for

Day 4: Something you consider beautiful

Day 5: Something you couldn't live without

Day 6: Your favourite place to chill out

Day 7: Something that you love

Describe, or draw a picture of your greatest accomplishment.

Find a quote that you love, one that reminds you what life is all about. Write it here:

RESILIENCE

'I put my newly learned skills to use, focusing on my breathing, keeping my mind in the present and experiencing where I was rather than ruminating on what might have been.'

Eoin Pluincéad

Ian Lacey

I first heard the words 'ulcerative colitis' in 2003.

'Ulcerative what?' I asked the consultant doctor at St Vincent's Hospital.

'It's an autoimmune disease of the colon,' he replied. 'You have ulcers in your large intestine but your body's defences are attacking them excessively, causing tissue damage. This is why you've developed such debilitating symptoms.'

For the previous three months I had experienced anaemia, constant diarrhoea, severe fatigue, and lost over three stone. I was already a thin 17-year-old, but at this point appeared a gaunt shadow of my former self. Complicating matters more, I was in Leaving Certificate year and had missed twenty-four days of school before Christmas. Now, just five months from my final exams, I was finally finding out what had drained every ounce of my physical and mental energy.

Fast-forward eight years and it's 2011. Fortunately, I passed my exams and made it to UCD where I completed both a bachelor's and a master's degree. Keeping me healthy was a strict regimen of medication which I took three times daily to keep the nasty symptoms of colitis away. In the intervening years, I suffered relapse just twice, meaning I returned to ill health briefly, but a course of steroids would bring my body back into balance and remission. However, my biggest challenge with the disease was yet to come.

In July 2011, I decided to ride my bicycle, unsupported, from Deadhorse, Alaska – the northernmost point accessible by road in the Americas – to Ushuaia, Tierra del Fuego, Argentina, the southernmost city in the world. This 27,000km journey would take me through some of the most remarkable environments on the planet, and offer me the opportunity to encounter the people and cultures that lived in them. I was cycling in aid of The Carers Association of Ireland, and in memory of my grandmother, who my family cared for in our Wexford home for almost twenty-four years.

With just two months until departure, the familiar symptoms of tiredness, concentration loss, regular visits to the bathroom, and most frighteningly of all, weight loss, were back.

I found myself in hospital again.

'I'm sorry to say you've relapsed, Ian,' the doctor said. 'I think you know what I'm going to say.'

I did. And in no way did I want to listen. He told me I should postpone the bike trip and try again next year.

'The symptoms should have dissipated by then and you'll feel better,' he told me.

This hurt. I had raised money for charity, built an immense support-base in my community, and had bought a new bicycle and the gear necessary to keep me warm, safe and self-reliant over the coming fifteen months. With such a small window of time to leave (twenty-four-hour darkness and a sub-zero Alaskan autumn and winter would soon sweep in), I felt, perhaps stupidly, it was now or never.

I rode out of Deadhorse, Alaska on 16 July 2011, excited for the waiting Americas but altogether incapable of cycling through them. If leaving my girlfriend and family wasn't tough enough already, the colitis was unremitting in its will to send me home. I was on a course of steroids for the previous six weeks but unlike the periods before, they hadn't taken effect.

My immediate geography wasn't going to help either. I was in the Arctic tundra, where dull greys and browns reflected my own desensitised mind. I was also over 800km from the nearest town of Fairbanks, the closest patch of urbanity with doctors and hospitals. One point of fortune was that I was cycling with my friend, Lee, and should anything go wrong, he'd be there as support, and to flag down a passing truck coming from the oil fields outside of Deadhorse.

Lee and I planned to ride 100km per day, meaning we'd arrive in Fairbanks in just over one week. We carried 40kg of gear, food and spare bike parts, so achieving this target would be incredibly difficult for first-time touring cyclists. On our first night, I rolled into my tent soaking wet and cold. A rainstorm had moved in over the previous two hours, christening our maiden voyage south. I felt intolerably sick and spent the night shivering uncontrollably inside my sleeping bag, aware that the weather was playing just a minor part in that. I swallowed another sachet of my medicine and wondered what I could possibly do to make it to Fairbanks. Even though I generally felt better in the mornings, by lunchtime I was going through hot and cold spells and my hands were shaking. Aside from this physical representation of the colitis, my mental health was suffering as much.

My thoughts were one-dimensional. I had no interest in the land I pedalled through, despite the fact I was one of a handful of travellers each year that got to see it. When the rain passed, the formerly grey expanse turned into a palette of deep greens and blues, and circular kettle lakes glinted brightly in the midday sun. Rare birdlife appeared over grassy hillocks and flew over us as we rode through one of the last great tracts of American wilderness. I, of course, couldn't have cared less about it. Only at that point did I realise that there would be no point continuing if I couldn't immerse myself in its majesty.

I made a pact with myself, a simple one. I would plan just for one day at a time. If I was to give my body any chance of beating the disease – putting it back in storage for a while – I could only do it with as positive an outlook as I could muster.

At the time, it seemed facetious to think I could lift my spirits just by 'thinking positively', but I set about this goal in a number of ways.

First, I concentrated on my revolutions. The only thing I had a semblance of authority over was the ability to turn the wheels. In essence, cycling became a form of meditation where one kilometre turned into two, then four, and so on. I concentrated on making the next kilometre until I reached the end of the day.

Second, I started talking to Lee about my illness. Once he appreciated that I couldn't climb a steep incline as fast as him, he'd wait at the top.

'Oh, come on, you're like a goddam snail getting up that. It's practically a molehill!' he'd say, making light of the situation.

'You've more power in those lanky Irish legs than you know of!' he'd finish off before racing away, encouraging me to catch him. Humour and laughter proved to be more powerful than I thought.

Lastly, I focused on my girlfriend Áine and my family back in Ireland. There had been worry behind their encouragement when leaving, and I was determined to change this. Instead of wondering when they'd receive the call I needed to come home, I wanted them wondering when they'd hear I'd crossed into a new country, had met intriguing characters, or ascended a snow-capped mountain in the Andes.

Gradually – very gradually – things got better. I'm not sure if it was down to my own resolutions, but I can't discount them. Why should I, even if it wasn't in line with the doctors' assertions of what would make me better?

We reached Fairbanks grotty and exhausted. Of primary concern was the shower, a facility we hadn't experienced the humble pleasure of in ten days. I can't say I felt great, but I didn't feel too bad either. We had taken a small, almost immeasurable bite out of 27,000km, but we had taken something, and that was an achievement in itself. If we could cycle 800km, then we could cycle 1,600km, and 3,200km, and so on again. My daily calculations added up to make weekly and monthly triumphs over what turned out to be a mental as well as physical malady. By the time we rolled into Vancouver, Canada, eighty-four days later, I had all but forgotten about counting, and instead was truly experiencing.

On 10 October 2012, my wheels turned for the last time in the city of Ushuaia, the magnificent terminus of the Pan-American Highway at the bottom of wild Patagonia. Four hundred and sixty-two days, through fifteen countries on two continents, and my long-held dream had been realised.

It would be remiss to say the ulcerative colitis didn't affect me again on the trip, but I was healthier and fitter than ever before, meaning its symptoms swiftly departed before they ever took hold. Today, I don't even take medication. What was once diagnosed as a lifelong disease (and I do still have it) is now under my own control. A proper diet, keeping active, and partially still living through my incredibly privileged journey continues to keep it at bay. And although I realise it could easily come back, I feel more equipped than ever to deal with it. I just hope that this time it doesn't involve fifteen months on a bicycle!

Vicky Kavanagh

I watched the minute hand make its way around the clock with a vacant expression, trying to match the pace of my breathing to time. My heart was beating as fast as the wings of a hummingbird. I stood up from the metal bench and walked over to the closed double doors. Peering through the glass inset, I watched as doctors and nurses worked on, and fussed around, my mum. Of her, all I could see were her feet, bare and limp. I watched as these strangers – who in that moment were the most important people in the world – tried to save my mum's life.

I had just turned 16 when my mum – my wonderful, vibrant, inspiring mother – was diagnosed with depression. At the time, I didn't know much about it. I'd heard the word used casually, trivially, before but never with regard to matters of life and death or matters of lasting consequence.

I'd noticed changes with my mum in the weeks before she was diagnosed; she was melancholy, exhausted, listless, and devoid of passion or enthusiasm. But given that my parents had just separated after a very difficult marriage, I thought it was normal. I mean, who wouldn't be sad in that situation? It was only as her behaviour became more despondent that I began to realise this wasn't normal. Then suddenly, without warning or invitation, the day arrived that changed my family's life forever.

Sitting outside that emergency room as doctors worked to save my mum, I was a bundle of emotions. I felt pure grief at what she had done, but I also felt angry at her, guilty for not seeing this coming, lost, helpless ... All I wanted to do was throw my head back and scream like a feral animal. My sister rushed down the hall, still dressed in her work clothes. We embraced in a hug, her arms wrapped tightly around me. In that moment we both felt very, very young.

My mum survived her suicide attempt, but it would not be her last. We had navigated the battle but the war still raged on. The war for my mum was the internal conflict she was suffering; the desperation, sadness and bleakness consuming her, the darkness that no light seemed capable of combatting. For me, my war was heart versus mind. I bounced between wanting to do anything – *anything* – that would make my mum feel better to feeling pure rage about what she had done. 'How could she want to leave us? How could she have been fine with us finding her that way?'

I thought, anger bubbling up inside me as if I were a kettle on a flame. I didn't know what to do; I didn't know how to help myself, my mum, my sister. It was like being alone in a thick forest, with no compass to guide me to safety.

For a while I used alcohol as a way to cope, as my crutch. I went out on the weekends and got wasted because my sister was home to keep an eye on my mum. More than once, I left my house on a Friday evening and didn't return until Sunday. These weekends were a haze of drinks, reckless behaviour, and doomed attempts to block out the frustration I felt at my life. I can honestly say there was never a single occasion when drinking made me feel better. At first, you're having a few drinks with your friends, you're dancing and laughing and feeling young. Then you keep drinking. The dancing becomes clumsy, the laughter too forced and high-pitched. You stop feeling young, and everything you were trying to escape comes rushing back with unwanted clarity. All I ever got from binge drinking were hangovers, and increasingly unstable emotions.

I believe the moment I began to grow up was not marked by a birthday or milestone; it was when I realised I *had* to stop what I was doing. I had to find a better way to deal with what was going on. There was no 'eureka' moment. I have no poignant story to offer of a single incident that made me stop turning my back on what was happening and instead face it head on. It occurred gradually, an accumulation of painful 'mornings after' forcing me to admit that I wasn't coping. I was spiralling out of control. I began using the internet to research depression, to better understand what my mum was going through. I have always believed that knowledge is power. If you want to slay a dragon, figure out how the dragon moves. I began to realise that my mum was suffering from an illness of the mind, the same way people suffer physical illness. She hadn't asked for this to happen to her and she had limited control over it. Reading about the environmental and biological causes of depression helped me understand what my mum was going through. I began to realise that her depression was not a personal attack on me; it didn't mean that she didn't love me. She was sick and she needed help. I love my mum unconditionally and always will. And when you see someone you love in pain, you're compelled to help them; you have to help them.

It wasn't easy but then again, life wasn't designed to be easy. Over the years, my mum has had periods when she was well, happy, jovial and playful. She's also had moments when the darkness would come back and envelop her. Most of these moments resulted in a suicide attempt; over the years, I've genuinely lost count of how many. Trying to get my mum to stick to a routine of therapy or counselling was incredibly difficult. There were times when you could see her dips coming and you went on high alert, knowing you were skating on cracked ice. There were moments when it seemed like nothing had ever happened. But whether she was in a good place or a bad place, her illness became a constant in our lives that we had to deal with.

After I realised alcohol was not the solution to my problems, I had to find a different way to cope with reality. I wouldn't be able to help myself, or my mum, if I didn't take care of my own mental health. The first thing I did was tell somebody what was going on. The words poured from me like the hiss of a balloon – sudden and rushing – and then relief poured over me in waves and I cried, great sobbing tears of grief and worry that I had contained for too long now poured out in a sweet release. Looking back, I wish I had told somebody sooner, but hindsight is a great thing; no bloody use when you're in the middle of a situation, but great for future learning. It was then that I learned talking about your problems didn't make you weak, it made you strong. Bottling up her feelings and problems allowed the monster of depression to get hold of my mum. Bottling up what was going on in my life made me turn to alcohol and do things I regret in a desperate bid to escape my life. But talking gives you strength and power. It provides clarity and focus and makes you realise you're not alone in this fight, and it is a fight you *can* and *will* win.

I always loved writing, so I began using it as a way to express myself. I poured my soul onto blank white pages that soon filled with the words of short stories, poems, or simply accounts of how I was feeling. It was cathartic and invigorating and each time left me feeling more able to handle whatever was happening. I found comfort in music and quotes, walking outside, and time with my friends.

As a result of my mum's illness my entire perspective on mental health changed. I began to recognise and respect its importance. My mental health wasn't something that would simply take care of itself, but something that needed to be protected and strengthened like the physicality of my body. I watched as my mum's attitude to mental health changed too. It took time, but she began to realise the intricacies of her illness, how it fed off silence and self-isolation. She forged her own tools to take up arms and began talking – to me, my sister, and professionals – about what she was going through. It took a while to get there, but watching her flower into the person she was before the depression once again is the most treasured memory I have.

It hasn't been an easy journey for any of us, nor is it a journey that has reached its conclusion, but my mum's depression is now a shadow rather than an overwhelming darkness in our lives. She has bad days, but we deal with them. I have moments when I feel like I can't carry on but I seek help, be it from my family, friends or another source. None of this process has been easy – learning to trust my mum again, fighting the paralysing fear when she has a bad day that she'll make another attempt on her life, worrying if she's on her own in the house – but it has taught me a lot. It's made me realise that I am stronger than I thought I could be, that I can move on from things that, at the time, I never thought I'd be able to get over. I've forged a happy and successful life, fulfilling my dream of working as a journalist, which at one time seemed inconceivable.

I'm a very different person to the one I was when I was 16. I'm now a woman who has stared into the darkness of humanity, but still believes in the light. I know that life is transient and that bad experiences do not define you. Your actions and responses, how you choose to live after the storm – that is what defines you. It's what shapes you into the person you are. My mum now knows that there is nothing *ever* so bad that you should take your own life. I know now that even when a person feels truly broken, no one is ever irreparably shattered.

I'm not a religious person and while I believe that there is some divine purpose to our lives, I do not look to the skies in my desperate moments. When I need a saviour, I look to my fellow man. It is people that save each other. It is people that make the longest day bearable, make you snort with laughter, hold your hand when you're scared.

We band together to share problems and joys, good moments and bad. There is always someone who will listen, someone who will help. I'm grateful for the fact that there is never a moment when we are truly alone. It's what saved me. It's what saved my mum. It's what we all need to remember, what we all need to believe. Just speak an honest sentence and go from there. You won't look back. You won't regret it.

Eoin Pluincéad

When I went to prom (yes, the American version of the Debs – how I ended up going to prom is a whole different story ...) back in 2005, I got to know a few of my date's friends. I stayed in touch with one of them on quite a regular basis and she and I grew very close over the intervening six years. Throughout our college years, we were always just an email away to provide support, share jokes and stories, and chat idly about the state of the world long into the night. With an ocean between us, however, we never thought we'd actually spend time together again. This prospect became even less likely when she moved to Los Angeles in the summer of 2010.

After a year of working, though, I had a nice nest egg saved up and decided to fly out to spend ten wonderful days together, seeing everything there was to see: Disneyworld, Santa Monica, The Hollywood Walk of Fame, Universal Studios, San Diego Zoo. I was also arriving just in time for Independence Day celebrations, which I had been promised would be amazing.

I landed in LA and she met me at the airport. We travelled to her apartment so I could sleep off the jet lag before beginning to explore the following morning. We spent a memorable morning together, chilling out at the beach before going to her friend's house for a Fourth of July barbecue. A little while into the party she rang her family to wish them a happy Independence Day. And that's when everything went pear-shaped.

My ten-day trip of a lifetime, entirely spontaneously planned, was cut short by nine days due to an unavoidable need for her to get 'back east' to her family. In the moment, my only focus was on making sure she was okay, while rescheduling my flights home, but as I sat in the airport the next morning at 5 a.m., the disappointment I had been warding off began to sink in.

As I was 5,000 miles from home, it was tough to come up with an effective coping strategy for what I was going through. I also had the added burden of feeling selfish for being upset. I kept reminding myself that everything happens for a reason and that, despite the absolute devastation I was feeling, no one had been grievously injured.

Initially, I found some comfort in plugging into music. Next, because I had recently taken part in a mindfulness course under the tutelage of Tony Bates and some Buddhist monks, I put my newly learned skills to use; focusing on my breathing, keeping my mind in the present and experiencing where I was rather than ruminating on what might have been.

All of my Irish friends knew how excited I had been about going, and so when I got back I decided to stay off the radar for the length of time that should have been my trip.

I let a small circle of people know the situation I was in and how I was feeling, which was much more productive than sending out a general message and having to field a barrage of 'how are you doing?'-style questions. It also gave me time to come to terms with what had happened and figure out how I was going to cope with it myself. Those who did know were very supportive of my de-stressing and my few days of peace.

During those days I found that the emotions weren't always overwhelming, but tidal – they would ebb and flow, and my need to deal with and consider them would increase and decrease in tandem. I had experienced a similar circadian emotion pattern a couple of years previously when I was attending counselling for major depression. Had I been unaware that such cycles occur I can only imagine how much harder it would have been to combat the feelings of anger, regret, disappointment, upset, and frustration as they flowed back when I had hoped that they had finished with me.

In those nine days off, I got the chance to enjoy my family and close friends' company without the pressures of 'normal' life. That really helped to remind me of what is important, and it gave me the personal space and time I needed to deal with what was happening in my body and my mind. It also went some way to making up for the opportunity missed. I guess what they say is true: each time a door closes, a window opens. It's important to always remember that, however difficult it might be.

I had, for so long, looked forward to a hypothetical, which – as rare as it is – became a reality. In retrospect, it seems folly to have placed those eggs in that basket. At the time, of course, it made perfect sense. The opportunity I got, though, from the apparent falling apart of worlds, has stood to me over time.

I still often reflect on what occurred, its rapidity, and its devastating impact in the moment. But now I can step back, take stock, and remember that I have been through hardship, relied upon others, and come out the far side happier, healthier and Okay. She and I don't speak any more – we corresponded briefly after I got home, but neither of us was able to face the massive mountain of emotion that had arisen between us. The proverbial elephant took over the room. Through mutual friends, I know she is doing well, and I'm glad of that.

The world, in the words of an author I admire, is not a wish-granting factory. This was the holiday of a lifetime, cut short by greater need. No one's wish was ultimately granted. But both she and I found within ourselves the strength we needed to get through the difficulties we faced. And we know that strength exists, should we need to draw upon it again.

Recently, I was reminiscing with an ex (from long ago, now a very good friend), and we recalled how the pain we felt when we broke up was like nothing – in that moment – anyone else in existence had ever felt. We were, of course, subjectively right. Objectively, though? Any disappointment, especially with a build-up, or a history, will hurt to the core. The key is to find healthy ways that suit you to cope with that pain. These were mine, in that moment, and they remain trusted to this day.

Caitrina Cody

Having a bad hair day? I know more about that than most people. When I was 20 years old, I lost my hair to a condition called alopecia. It's actually fairly common, with more than eight million women in the UK (Irish statistics are hard to find) experiencing it at some point in their life.

What happened was a shock to me, my friends and my family. It's just not really what you expect, is it? As I continued to lose more and more of my long, curly hair, it became clear that this was going to significantly affect my life for some time.

Halfway into my second year of college, it almost felt like the end of the world. I wasn't the most confident of people to start with, and adapting to life in UCD had already proved incredibly stressful, as is the case for many. I was entering uncharted territory, and rather than worrying about what to wear or where to sit in lecture theatres, I was busy trying to disguise large bald patches on my head from people sitting behind me.

Everyone had a well-meaning piece of advice to offer. One friend of the family had a sister who'd lost her hair, but she'd gotten it all back within a year. Another relative had lost hair while pregnant, but that had turned out to be temporary. So whatever I did, I shouldn't lose hope. Surely someone could fix this.

I'll never forget the day I went to see my local GP. I felt a bit silly, because it wasn't like I was sick or anything. There was nothing physically wrong with me, except – whoops! – my dodgy hair follicles didn't seem to be able to do their job and hold on to my hair for me.

At this stage, I was alternating between feeling incredibly sorry for myself and feeling like I was overreacting to something that, on the scale of things, was relatively minor. Some days it felt like all I was missing in reality was a big bunch of split ends. Other days it felt like my entire identity.

My doctor, a cheerful, straight-talking kind of guy, looked at my scalp, examined the large patches of bare skin and asked me the usual series of routine medical questions. He admitted that he wasn't too familiar with alopecia and made an appointment for me at the dermatology unit of a Dublin hospital, before pledging to do some research himself. Finally, just as I was getting ready to leave, he fixed me with a steady gaze. He reminded me that because nobody knows for definite what causes alopecia, no treatment is guaranteed to work, then he said that for the good of my mental health, I should probably resign myself to the possibility of never having hair again. Forgetting about my hair altogether, he added, was the best thing I could do right now.

Harsh words. My heart sank, but I met his gaze and nodded before leaving the room and numbly paying my bill. Over the next few days, my feelings of shock at his statement mounted into anger and denial. How could he say something like that? He was a doctor, I'd gone to him for help and all he could tell me to do was to admit defeat.

What followed were intensive internet searches on every possible cure for alopecia, from immunotherapy (suppressing your immune system so it can't prevent your follicles from producing hair) to acupuncture. For quite a while I continued to hope that someone would fix my problem for me, that I could take a pill or injection, or try a new vitamin or treatment that would restore my hair to its former glory.

Reading the online forums dedicated to alopecia can be heartbreaking. So many people spend years of their life and large chunks of their savings on laser treatment and expensive drugs, none of which prove to be that effective usually.

I read stories of women who wore wigs every day of their life and wouldn't even let their husbands see them without one, much less leave the house.

What I had wanted from my doctor was hope that some of these treatments would work for me, not encouragement to resign myself to my lot, but he was firm enough not to give the 20-year-old girl standing in front of him any false hope, and I'm grateful for that.

Somewhere over the years that have since passed, the truth of his words sank in and I began to gently slide what had happened to the side and move on with my life.

It didn't happen overnight. And events didn't help. When my hair grew back a year later, I was delighted, and my family and friends praised me as though I'd done it myself through sheer positive thinking, not like it was a weird cellular anomaly over which I had no control. But at the back of my mind, my GP's words still resonated softly, reminding me that if my fortunes changed again, I had to be ready to face it.

Looking back, I think he was preparing me for the hard times that he knew would be likely to come my way. Sure, if my hair grew back and stayed put, I could scornfully dismiss his pessimism and walk off into the sunset, shaking my lustrous locks in victory, but I like to think the message behind his words was not to let the loss of my hair define me, to work on building my life without it, so that I could survive and be happy regardless.

I think that's why, when it all fell out again within two years, it wasn't the crushing blow it could have been. In a weird twist, I found myself consoling my family and friends and trying to show them I was okay – that really, the worst had happened once again, and I was all right.

There have been massive ups and downs along the way. I've found myself capable at times of being utterly okay with my hair as it now is – shorn, white and fairly straggly at the back – to the point that I'll walk confidently around the city, proud of how I look.

And I'll also have moments where I'll walk around in a paranoid daze, feeling like people in the supermarket are giving me strange looks. I'll feel almost guilty for possibly confusing people and anxious that I'm attracting negative attention.

There have been two light-bulb moments in recent years that have really made a difference to me. They occurred with the help of my boyfriend, who has always loved my hair the way it is and has never known me any other way.

The first is the realisation that I don't need to apologise to anyone for the way my hair looks. Sure, it can look weird sometimes, depending on the way the wind blows. And yes, it can be surprising for people to meet me one day wearing long brown wig, and the next with short, white, patchy hair.

But that's okay: confusing people is not a crime. If I feel like explaining, then by all means, if you have a spare hour or two, I can happily tell you my life story. But if I'm not in the mood? I'll leave it to you to figure out for yourself.

The second is the realisation that most of the time, people are not even looking at me. I go through my life, mostly concerned on a day-to-day basis with my own issues and the concerns of the people I love. I'm assuming the majority of other people do the same.

Of course it's important to care about other people on a social level and to engage with what's going on around you, but on a personal, emotional level, as we all go about our business – in the supermarket, on the bus, in college – we're all wrapped up in our own immediate moments to some extent.

So when I go around the supermarket anxiously assuming that everyone is eyeing me with distaste, it's an entirely futile, frustrating waste of energy. I'll never know what other people are thinking about me (if anything) and I don't need to know. What I do know and can control, with practise, is how I feel about myself, so that's where I try to expend my energy these days.

But whether I'm having a good, self-confident, I-have-no-hair-and-I-don't-care day or a moment in which I would literally prefer to put a paper bag over my head than face the world, I try not to blame myself for any of my feelings.

There are advantages to having alopecia. Not many people can have a different hairstyle to match various outfits and it only takes me about half an hour to get ready for work in the morning. The world of GHDs and hair dye is a long-lost memory and one I am happy to forget.

Sometimes I wonder what advice I would give to my 20-year-old self. I wonder what I'd say if I had to personally break the news to her that she'd be going through her twenties without the hair she'd counted on having. There's no shortcut to these things, though, and no magic wand; so nothing I could tell her would make losing her hair easier to bear. These things just have to be worked out along the way, with support from the people around you.

One thing I would tell her is to learn to laugh at herself and the situation as much as she can. There's a funny side to everything, and cracking jokes about raising my eyebrows (if I had any) and feigning anguish when my friends mention their new haircuts has definitely helped to ease the sting along the way.

Losing my hair taught me a lot about myself and I don't regret what happened for a second. It's an old adage but a true one: what doesn't kill you makes you stronger. The people who know and love me know me for the person I am today. That person wouldn't be the same had I not been formed by my struggles along the way, as every person inevitably is.

Activity

My greatest strengths are ...

The person that inspires me most is ...

The biggest obstacle I have overcome in my life
so far is ...

The smartest choices I have made:

1.

2.

3.

My greatest achievements of the past year
have been ...

1.

2.

3.

CONNECT

'My online video "confession" made something both amazing and heartbreaking happen.'

Eoghan McDermott

Sinéad Desmond

My job involves getting up at an ungodly hour as I co-anchor a three-hour live breakfast show, TV3's *Ireland AM*, every day of the week. People always ask me how I cope with the early mornings but I really don't mind them that much. I'm lucky because I'm a morning person. I'm also lucky to have buckets of energy; if truth be known, I'm quite hyperactive and, if anything, I find winding down difficult but most nights I manage to drift off by about ten.

The best part of my job is not the talking, which I do a lot of – far too much of most of the time – it's the listening. It's a very artificial scenario, the television sofa, so your job is to make someone feel at ease and to let them know they can trust you to help them to get their story across. Of course everyone is different: one interviewee could be a world-famous actor, the next a mum or dad or even a child who has overcome extraordinary obstacles. People often thank me after these interviews, but I always feel it should be the other way around – I want to thank them. I feel privileged that someone would share their story with me. People bare their souls to you and to the viewers and nine times out of ten they are doing it to try to help others. It's a brave thing to do.

So much has happened on the *Ireland AM* sofa in the time that I have been there. I suffered a brain haemorrhage, live on air, back in 2008. I felt a cramp in my neck while reading the newspaper headlines to camera, and my vision began to go a bit funny. I was taken off air and was rushed to Beaumont Hospital, where the brilliant medical team ensured I was one of the fortunate ones not to suffer any lasting side effects – no negative ones, anyway. Actually, if anything it had a positive effect on me. I was always a *carpe diem* kind of girl but since that incident I have really worked hard to make sure I am getting the most out of everything that I am doing, and to be as healthy as I possibly can be. I exercise, take a stupid amount of supplements, glug down green juices and all the other stuff you should do, and it works. I'm feeling better than I ever have.

The truth is that I have never had a problem looking on the bright side, or making the most of a bad situation: it has come naturally. I've always been the girl who thinks things will work out in the end. Sure, I've had some really challenging periods in my life, but nothing compared to some people, and no matter how bad it gets I always believe everything will work out in the end. And do you know what? It always does. Being a naturally optimistic person is a real gift, and one that I am very thankful for, but of course there are days when everything seems hard and you just need a hug. Thankfully I have great people in my life who are there when things are tough.

Coping when things are difficult is a mental health issue, but how we feel on a daily basis is also a mental health issue. That is something I have come to understand. We are all responsible for our mental health. If we don't mind it, we will face difficulties. As a journalist, I have written on the subject, seen the effects that mental health difficulties can have on individuals, families, even whole communities. And as wide a topic as mental health is, I was pretty sure I 'got it', but it's only in hindsight that I realise I never truly comprehended the depths of desperation people can feel. I could empathise, of course, but if I'm honest there was always a part of me that felt people could choose to feel differently. And I always struggled with the issue of suicide – I simply could not fathom why someone would choose to reject life and opt for death – but working on the *Ireland AM* Mental Health Awareness week changed all of that. It helped me to truly understand how those struggling with mental health issues feel and the challenges they face.

As part of the awareness week, I conducted a special series of interviews with well-known figures who had all battled with their mental health. These were household names: people like the author Marian Keyes, radio DJ Gareth O'Callaghan and GAA football star Alan O'Hara. From the outside, they appeared to have great lives. They were talented, successful, well liked and respected and they were well off. Many would think theirs were lives to envy and yet I discovered that underneath it all they shared experiences of barely keeping it together, and actively contemplating ending it all.

Of course in my personal life I'd been there for friends or family members who were feeling stressed, or perhaps depressed. Here, however, was a group of people laying themselves bare, and revealing the most intimate of details about their lives, and the difficulties that they had faced. The sort of stuff most of us would rather take to the grave than say to anyone, let alone share with the nation. Listening to them was an incredible experience. Their honesty was remarkable and they never shied away from the truth, no matter how bleak that was. Their stories were all unique, yet their voices united: each person was so very glad to be alive today. They had learned coping mechanisms, had hung on to each day, each hour, with all their might. Their message to anyone feeling as they have done? Just hang on.

But the real power in what they told me was simply the fact that they had chosen to tell their story. Instead of hiding their experience from themselves and everyone around them, they dragged it out into the light. By breaking that taboo, by talking about how they had all come so close to ending it all – not just thinking dark thoughts but taking real steps to finish their lives – they triumphed over their darkest times and helped others to see that it is possible to overcome them. They were all so brave, and so generous, to tell me the things they did. They all told their stories for one reason and one reason only: to help others.

And they helped others like me to understand what it is like to be in that black hole of depression, convinced there is no way out. Of course I will never truly know unless I go through it myself, but now I understand that you cannot choose to just pull your socks up and shake off feelings like that. I now fully appreciate how hard it is to speak out and get help when suffering a mental health crisis. And I think there are things that we can do to help. Instead of hoping that someone will reach out for help, why not reach out to them ourselves? It can be very difficult for someone to open up when they are in a dark place, so why not create a chink of light by saying, 'How are you doing?' Telling a friend, gently, that you are worried for their welfare is important. Okay, so they might tell you to sod off, but all you've endured is a bit of social embarrassment and chances are that if you're feeling concerned, there's a good reason for that.

Of course if you do have serious concerns for someone don't just go stumbling into it. Reaching out to such people requires some homework. Make it your mission to understand issues surrounding mental health. The information is there (ReachOut.com), and it's for everyone, not just those struggling with mental health issues. You can learn how to speak to someone who you are concerned about. In my experience, finding a quiet place and telling someone you love them and are worried about them is a good place to start. Simply meaningfully asking 'Are you all right?' and letting someone know you are there for them can often open up the conversation.

Remember, too, how deceptive appearances can be. If your friend seems like a great talker, that doesn't mean he or she doesn't have tricky stuff going on in the background. I'd even go so far as to say that a great communicator, someone who can talk their way around the houses, is often doing so because they don't want to talk about how they really feel!

I hope I'm getting better when it comes to understanding mental health, and I've promised myself I'll reach out to people whenever my gut instinct tells me it's the right thing to do. I'm also more protective than ever of my own mind, and a crappy day at work means I must go for a run or walk later on – it's not an option, it's a *must*. I know everyone bangs on about the need to exercise, but consider this: doctors are now actually prescribing exercise for depression. And they do this for one simple reason: it works! So my greatest single tool to help keep my mental health in good shape is exercise: running, swimming or going to the gym is my therapy.

Personally when things are hard I also find the phrase 'this too shall pass' very comforting. I remember the first time this helped me. When I began life as a newspaper journalist I remember the panic and rush of nerves that accompanied writing my first big news piece as I typed away under a fast-approaching deadline with my editor reading over my shoulder. I doubted my ability to do it. I sat at the keyboard, totally stressing out, feeling like I couldn't cope, until I reminded myself that in an hour, it would all be over. And it was. I wrote the piece and it was good.

So no matter how you're feeling right now, it's not permanent. All things change. All things pass. This too shall pass, and better things will – I promise! – come your way.

Eoghan McDermott

So here's what happened. The people at Pieta House, the centre for the prevention of self-harm or suicide, were organising a charity run, and they needed to drum up some advance media attention. It's a funny thing, really, that people 'off the telly' can help a charity maximise their newspaper coverage, but it's the way it goes, and being on *The Voice of Ireland* at the time led to a request for my involvement. This was an invitation I was more than happy to accept.

The day of the launch arrived, and with it came questions from the press. A journalist asked me the obvious: 'What prompted you, Eoghan, to become involved with Pieta House?' I told her it was because my mom had worked as a Home School Liaison, which is basically a social worker for a school. I explained that mom had opened my eyes to issues surrounding self-harm and suicide, and I had seen how her work had helped families ravaged by mental health difficulties. That sounded like a fairly appropriate response, didn't it?

Appropriate it may have been, and hey, it was technically the truth, but it wasn't the whole truth. The real reason this event resonated with me was because I used to self-harm. So I had two options: stay schtum and keep this information to myself, or throw it out there and, y'know, see what happened. I chose option number two.

Double-clicking the record button, I spoke to the camera on my PC for five minutes and forty-eight seconds. I talked about how, at twenty-six, I had found myself at the tail end of a five-year relationship. This relationship had been bright and rosy for several years, but when that person emigrated our attempts at maintaining a long-term relationship disintegrated. We broke up, and it really affected me. I remember how it felt, like a tidal wave coming along and smashing me over: all these ideas about my sense of self were scattered all over the place and I was desperately trying to cling onto them. Good friends guessed something was up, but when they tried to talk to me I would withdraw back into myself, refusing to volunteer any details. Instead of sharing these unfamiliar emotions I was bottling everything up, and my feelings were threatening to drown me.

The weird thing was that I knew that a break-up was not a disaster in the grand scheme of things, and I also knew that I was incredibly lucky to be surrounded by healthy and happy friends and family. I knew work was going well, too, and perhaps that compounded my confusion as to why I was feeling down. In retrospect, I suppose I had never experienced real emotional turmoil, or major hardships, before that time, and so this uncharted territory was proving tricky to navigate. My private coping mechanism, I told the camera, was to self-harm.

It was something I had never said out loud before. Self-harming, I explained, had felt like a rational, normal thing to do. It was a short-term, concentrated thing, and as I was living on my own at the time my family didn't have a chance to pick up on the problem. Removing yourself from people can be achieved quite easily, I'd found: y'know, say you're busy with work or whatever.

Thankfully, this time passed. I was lucky: those great friends and family I told you about helped me get back on track without realising it. I didn't seek professional help, yet hindsight tells me it would have been the smarter move. I now understand that self-harm is not something to be dealt with alone. It is not a rational response to an emotional issue; it's an irrational act that directly suggests you need some help. Self-harm is an abnormal manifestation of emotional turmoil, but very normal people – like me! – can and do experience it. My message now? Reach out and tell somebody!

In time I also came to terms with the end of my relationship. Speaking with a colleague who had experienced the heartache of a long-term romance helped; my discussions with her allowed me make sense of what had gone wrong and why. Today I stick with the Irish motto: '*Tiocfaidh sé nuair a thagann sé*' ('It will happen when it happens'). I reckon you can apply this thinking to any area of your life, from work to relationships, and it certainly reassures me that things will happen as they should and in their own good time.

My online video 'confession' made something both amazing and heartbreaking happen. Soon after posting it, all these people came out of the woodwork to share their stories with me. A member of my extended family revealed their struggle with depression, while a 15-year-old girl emailed me to say she had been contemplating suicide. She told me that my video had encouraged her to keep going, because if I could move on from a dark place then perhaps she could too. Another girl I know only socially took me by complete surprise. She is a very beautiful and highly successful model, and yet here she was, telling me this horrific story of her own experience of self-harm. Trust me: if you saw this girl you'd never believe her story, and it goes to show that anyone can have an adventure in mental health.

Their confessions made my confession feel worthwhile, and I hope that telling the truth was as cathartic for them as it has been for me. Who knew 'fessing up could feel so good?

Harriet Parsons

As Services Coordinator with Bodywhys, The Eating Disorders Association of Ireland, I often have very varied days. In my role, both as the link between the volunteers on our support services, and directly on the support services myself, I witness monumental turning points in people's lives, while the rest of the world continues to turn.

As I settle down at my desk I get a helpline call from a mum who is desperate to know how to approach her daughter, who in the past couple of months has lost an extreme amount of weight, and is severely restricting her diet. The mother is full of fear and her desperation is palpable on the call. She is at a loss to know what to do. Her daughter is in her mid-twenties; she is an adult, but is living at home and is out of work. The mother has tried talking to her, but, as she explains, her daughter refuses the mother's attempts to talk about what is going on. The mother is feeling helpless; she doesn't know how to 'get through' to her daughter or what she can do.

I talk to her about trying to understand that the eating issue could be her daughter's way of coping with how her life is for her at the moment. When I make this tentative suggestion, the mother agrees, and I know that in her heart of hearts this is not a new idea but rather something she has been unable to articulate. Her fear about her daughter's health has stopped her from being able to articulate this, but it means that there is no 'quick fix'. We talk about this. We talk about the approaches she has taken up until now, and this reflection allows the mother to realise that there is an opportunity to try a different approach, one that is not solely focused on what her daughter is doing, but rather focuses on how her daughter is feeling. We talk about having realistic expectations for any approach she tries, and we think about how it might be to have the expectation that, at this stage, the mother's goal might be to open of a line of communication rather than coming to a decision about what to do.

The mother feels relief, and can recognise that taking the pressure to do something specific off will allow her to communicate in a supportive way with her daughter. Towards the end of the call I gently ask the mother how she is coping with this, and at that point her tears flow freely and I can hear the change in her voice that the relief of talking brings. We end the call with a plan of sorts, but more importantly with an understanding that creating a sense of safety will be key to supporting her daughter to talk about what she is going through and making any decisions about how to get help to move on from this.

At this point, I check in with our volunteer support group facilitators who had been facilitating groups the night before. It turns out that in our city centre 'eating disorder' group there were seven people: four women and three men, four of whom had been to groups before. The facilitators talk about the support that was given by participants to each other at the group, and how the regular attendees were of huge support to the new people. At the beginning of the group one new person felt that she couldn't speak, but by the end she opened up and felt safe enough to talk about what she was going through.

In the 'family and friends' group, there were two sets of parents, and a husband. All spoke of different situations but gave each other great support in knowing that the recovery process is just that: a process, with ups and downs. I am always amazed at the courage of people attending the group, embracing the unknown and having the courage to explore the idea that there might be other people who can relate to them and to whom they can relate. An eating disorder is essentially an extremely personal experience, and it takes huge courage to think that someone else will be able to relate to one's story, and what one is going through.

In addition to the support groups in Dublin city centre last night, there was also an online support group running. In this group there were twelve participants, all of whom were able to relate to each other about topics such as family not recognising the change that they are experiencing and the pressure they feel from the people around them to change more quickly. As I read through the report from the online group, I think of the mother whom I had been talking to and I think about how an eating disorder affects relationships with family and friends. It acts as a barrier, keeping the person locked into the thinking of the eating disorder, and not allowing anyone else to understand it so that its distorted logic will not be challenged. I think about how being able to articulate what is going on in the person's head is the key to being able to challenge the thinking that supports the eating disorder, and it is also the key to helping family and friends understand what is going on and what it is like for the person.

On our helpline on this day, there was a call from a husband who was extremely concerned about his wife, who is in her forties and is refusing any help at all. There was a call from a mum of a 13-year-old boy, who had been called names in school a few months back and had stopped eating as a result. There was a call from a woman in her thirties who is currently in counselling for bulimia, and is finding things very difficult at the moment. And there was a call from a girl in her early twenties who has never told anyone that she makes herself sick a couple of times a day, and wanted to tell someone. All of these calls come from real people who have picked up the phone on this particular day for a particular reason and want to tell someone about what is going on.

As I log the statistical information for these calls, I check in on our email support service and there are four emails waiting to be answered. There is a woman who is in her thirties and has been dieting for a year. She feels things have gotten out of her control and now she is binging every day when her husband is at work. There is an email from a friend, who thinks that a girl she is living with is making herself sick at night-time and is binging when she is alone, and she doesn't know how to talk to her. There is an email from a 13-year-old girl who has anorexia and is really struggling with her treatment and feels that nobody understands her. And there is an email from a woman who is thanking us for a reply we sent her and says that it has made her think about her eating habits in an entirely different way. She is finding the courage to get help for herself.

This is a snapshot of just one of my working days. In a small way, I feel connected with all of these people. I feel it a privilege to be part of their story in some small way. I admire each and every one of them for picking up the phone, or writing an email, or going to a group.

Would I be able to do the same if I were in their shoes?
I don't know. I wonder about the kind of difference the
contact with our organisation has made for them that day,
the following day, and in the coming weeks. I do not know
how any of these stories will turn out. As I shut down my
computer, I hope that all will be well in their worlds, in their
lives, but I must come back tomorrow not knowing and
being satisfied with the not knowing. However, I have come
to treasure this not knowing because not knowing means
that I never assume I know what any one person ought to do
and instead it allows me to listen to them, it allows me to give
them the space to tell me what it is like for them, and it allows
me to equip them with the information and a supportive,
listening ear to do something for themselves. We talk about
turning points, about moments that change our lives, and on
any one day in the work I do, this is happening for people
over and over again. At least that is the hope that I have.

Tara Ní Mhóráin

Even though a lot of my friends and acquaintances have
moved on to greener pastures abroad, emigration had never
touched on my life in any massively meaningful way. I never
saw it on the cards for myself – too fond of my home com-
forts, possibly a bit too lazy as well – and I was never really
interested in going 'away' anywhere (unless there was going
to be a big Penneys!) When I was in college, these emigration updates would be highly publicised with headlines like,
'This many young people left the country since the last time
we checked'. I read about these poor unfortunates and my
heart went out to them and all their mammies who'd be
worried sick at home, wringing their hands at the thought of
their young one going out with wet hair. I never thought that
I might become one of those poor young ones venturing way
out to the foreign unknown, but I did.

When I was just about to finish a master's, I applied for a whole rake of jobs that didn't match my skill set, jobs I wasn't qualified for and had no interest in. Everyone does it! Jobs are a bit thin on the ground and I knew that there would be other people – possibly better than me – jostling for a bit of the job action. Also, I got a bit carried away when Dundalk Credit Union were looking to know when suited me to start paying back my student loan and in doing so frightened the life out of me.

About six months into this mad job hunt, I got a 'You have been selected for interview!!!' email. I was just about to mark the email as spam because of the heavy-handed punctuation when I winced as I realised what it was about. Oh God, not *that* job. I applied for it as my 'if I'm still in dire straits in a year's time, I'll take it' job. At this early and optimistic stage, I was still backing a few other job-horses and hoping one of them would cash in. I half-heartedly accepted the invitation for interview anyway, so that I could use it as a dress rehearsal for a job that I did want. Over the next few months, I continued to jump through various hoops for this job that I didn't really want: filling in forms, another interview, an exam, a trip over to see them in their foreign land, a medical exam, more forms, all the while hoping that another job, any other job, would come up.

Then the unthinkable happened: they offered me the job – in this faraway foreign land that no one goes to. I was painfully aware that I was in no position to be turning down a job, but it didn't stop me voicing my reluctance at taking this one. I had a few applications pending elsewhere which I really was hoping would come to something. When the last job on my wish list knocked me back with a rejection e-mail, I accepted the job and booked a one-way flight in a bit of a disappointed flurry, not fully appreciating the gravity of the situation.

My reservations about leaving Ireland are well-documented and were given a good airing before I left, too – just in case there were any prospective employers cheekily eavesdropping – but nobody else was flinging any jobs in my direction. As D-day got ever closer, there was this awful wave of panic rising from my stomach to my chest and up to my throat. I had a bit of trouble swallowing solid food anytime I thought about leaving. Food had a bit of a funny taste to it as well, a bit like dead leaves – but no one else ever complained so I presume that the food was actually fine and it was the paralysing worry making my imagination run riot. In waves it would wash over me, over and over again. 'I'll have to leave here, I'll be so far away ...'

And so the crying began.

These sad, salty tears would escape my eyes before I'd even have time to tell them to settle themselves. I could be casually catching up with my best friend over a coffee, she'd turn her back to throw away her chewing gum, and by the time she'd be facing me again I'd be blubbing like a baby. Similarly, I'd be driving to the shops with my mam and big fat tears would roll silently down my face. I'd try not to draw too much attention to myself and let them get on with it, rolling down my neck.

On the very last night I spent at home, I stared up at the ceiling and asked for some kind of divine intervention. I reasoned with the Almighty that seeing as I had just gotten my Irish driving licence, it wouldn't be practical for me to leave at this crucial stage of my driving career. I asked for some kind of intercession on this basis but He still has to get back to me on that one. Very busy man, I gather.

So with no intervention – divine or otherwise – it was time to go. My boyfriend came with me, to carry bags and mind me in my delicate emotional state. We spent a few nice days together, taking in the tourist sites before it was time for him to go home and for me to start work, find an apartment and start putting a life together. I didn't have much enthusiasm for any of these endeavours, but I threw myself into them with such dogged determination I could have given myself an injury. I got myself out of bed and presented for work every morning, introduced myself to my colleagues, found and moved into an apartment in a hyper-efficient blur.

Every so often I'd call home when I'd start to wilt and needed a pep talk. Sometimes I'd get a bit of tough love from my mam, sometimes I'd get the 'Ah now pet, you'll be grand' I was looking for, but the call would inevitably end with me sobbing uncontrollably down the phone, gulping about how much I wanted to come home.

Ticking things off my to-do list opened a whole new can of worms that I wasn't really expecting. This can of worms was full of commitment issues: signing a contract at work was a big one, as was signing for my apartment, another involved taking responsibility for the electricity and gas bills, as well as the internet, and yet another concerned my civil responsibility in this weirdly obedient land. The responsibilities piled up, each new one turning me into a bit of a crying mess. I don't want to be tied to anything here, I'd think. I don't want to leave too much of a mark. I just want to get out as soon as I can. My mentality when I first arrived was to not really engage in a social life, partly because I have a perfectly good one at home and partly because I wanted to believe that the less I have here, the easier it will be when I do get to go home. Even though I don't know when that will be.

I'm finding the evenings and the weekends very tough over here. I have to stop myself from climbing into bed at 9 p.m. and try to stay up a bit later because for a while there, I'd wake at 5 a.m. fully rested and have to wait for ages before it was okay to get up. And it really is the most awful feeling waking really early on a Saturday morning and wishing it were already Monday again so I could be surrounded by the people and noise that help me forget that I've no friends and that all I want to do is go home. Also, it's slightly less okay to cry for prolonged periods while you're supposed to be engaged in gainful employment. In the evenings it's just me and my mind and all the privacy in the world to bawl my eyes out. So I've started to busy myself with making a decent dinner for myself – it takes longer than a non-decent dinner and it tastes a bit nicer as well. Hopefully some of my friends might come out here and visit me and I can show off my new recipe book and all the dinners I know how to make now. Who knows? They might be so impressed by my new domesticity that they won't want to go home – then I can have a friend to play with all the time!

My initial plan of not getting involved in a social life here had to be revised so I joined a few clubs – including a GAA one, for the first time in my life – and I'm starting to meet other people in a similar situation to me: new in town, lonely, a bit lost. It was such an amazing relief to meet a few people who know what I'm going through and want to talk about it. At first, I thought I was going to feel like this forever, or how-ever long I am to be 'exiled' here, but I'm meeting people now that have recovered from the initial trauma of waving goodbye to all they've known and assure me of their happy and well-adjusted lives here now. I take enormous comfort from that and can only hope that I'll be telling the same story as them in a short while. In the meantime, I'm taking baby steps, I'm getting to know my neighbourhood and what the nightlife is like. I'm exploring this new country and enjoying learning about its culture and history. I'm learning to be a bit kinder to myself and learning how to be happy and comfort-able here. Unexpectedly, I've found out that I'm a lot braver than I thought I was.

Katie Kelly

The music was thumping in the background as the sound of laughter filtered in through the cubicle door. No one had any idea what was going through her mind. Even she didn't really realise what she was doing, or thinking. But something had driven her over the edge and nothing was going to stop her dragging the glass across her wrist. Her mind was clouded by the vodka, and her emotions were running wild. It was now or never.

This may sound like an episode of *Skins*, or *Dawson's Creek*, or some other over-the-top teenage drama series, but unfortunately this is based on real life, and an event that made its way into in my life recently.

Let's just say there is a dingy bar in town with a certain 'reputation'. I go there frequently; it's kind of habit at this stage. It's just where my friends and I have always gone, and nothing is going to change that.

But the other week, when this incident occurred, my mind was on overdrive. The situation, I thought, had gotten out of control. I was standing outside the ladies, obeying a call of nature. Unusually, there was a bouncer on the door (it's not normally *that* bad ...). In my own drunken state, I was demanding to be let into the bathroom, but all the worried-looking bouncer kept saying was: 'There's a problem. You will have to wait.' Well, my bladder isn't as young as it used to be, so I promptly made my way to the men's, and back to the bar. It was only then that I noticed the paramedics go into the ladies.

Of course the first thing that entered my mind, and I'm sure the minds of many others, was that there had been a fight, or perhaps someone had availed of too many cheap drinks, or decided to experiment with drugs. Each of the above are common practice within this particular establishment.

I continued on with my night, forgetting about the paramedics until a friend of mine told me the truth: a girl had been carried out on a stretcher, having slashed her wrists. And, to top it all off, the word was that things like this happen all the time here. My friend simply brushed it off as another stupid teenager looking for attention in a rock bar. How typical.

But I can't brush these things off. I couldn't stop myself wondering what had driven this girl to carry out such a terrible act on herself. Who had found her? Had this happened previously? And, of course, would she be okay?

It's the age-old case of teenagers and young people drinking too much. On this night in particular there were drinks promotions galore, and the crowd was very young (which made me feel very old).

I remember my teenage years fondly, but I know that when alcohol is involved it can get messy. There were many tears and fights, and a lot of shouting and drama, but nothing ever escalated to the point where someone genuinely wanted to take their own life.

Society will be society, and it may blame this incident on hormones or drinking, but there was obviously an underlying issue with this girl, just as with many teenagers. Maybe sometimes this kind of self-harming behaviour is brushed under the carpet, with the justification that it's just 'another stupid girl drinking too much and getting overly emotional about some boy', etc.

The fact is that if someone commits such a violent act against themselves in a pub, surrounded by people, something is just as wrong as it would be if it had happened in their own home.

I've been thinking about the girl quite a lot since it happened. I have no idea who she is, but I can't help but feel a sort of affinity with her. We were all young once, and I reckon we were all depressed at least once during the tumultuous teenage years. Some of us were just lucky that it never got so out of hand. I don't think it's fair to judge people like her. Judgement leads to ridicule, which only make matters even worse.

It's time for teenagers suffering with depression to be taken just as seriously as their adult counterparts. Otherwise, incidents like this will increase, and the already staggering suicide rate amongst young people will rise. Mine was just one night out, remember, and that was just one girl.

Activity

Choose one of these random acts of kindness and make it happen in the next week:

Buy a coffee for a friend

Offer to do the washing up

Bring cookies to school or work
(everybody loves cookies!)

Leave a note for someone you love
telling them why they are great!

Or come up with your own random act or kindness.

Talk to a friend about a new hobby you'd like to take up together ... Write about it here:

BE

'I need to remind myself regularly that downtime is a requirement, that switching off is something I need to do in order to be happy.'

Alan Quinlan

Alan Quinlan

Feeling under pressure? I built a career on it. As a professional rugby player I lived the dream, playing for Munster and for Ireland, and it was ... well, it was amazing. There were spectacular highs, and I remember the personal sense of purpose that accompanied doing my province and my country proud.

I retired from rugby in 2011. There are elements I miss, of course – my teammates and the banter, the big matches, and of course the big wins. However, pressure was also part of the game – the butterflies in your belly before kick-off, the media attention surrounding how you and your team performed on any given day. This pressure was something I was not ideally equipped to deal with and it is an aspect of being a professional sportsman that I can now say I do not miss.

Let me start by saying this: I haven't had an unhappy life; it's been brilliant so far. I am, however, a naturally anxious person, prone to worry and negative thinking. Pressure can get on top of me – it has got on top of me at certain times. There have been days when I wouldn't want to get out of bed, days when all I could do was silently worry about all sorts of things – mostly things that were never likely to happen. I could and did perform well in huge arenas, packed with tens of thousands of supportive, cheering fans. These onlookers considered me a happy, confident and positive person, no doubt. Sure, how could they see the truth behind my stuck-on smile?

As a young person I didn't understand the term 'mental health'. I thought feeling anxious was something I simply had to endure, alone. I have a wonderful family, but never told them how I was feeling. Instead, I played rugby, and did the macho thing of never revealing my fears or emotions to anyone. It wasn't until I neared retirement from professional sport that it dawned on me: the time had come to let my guard down.

My autobiography, *Red-Blooded*, afforded me the opportunity to reflect on my life and the choices I've made. It also presented a challenge: would I write with honesty, or gloss over the facts? I decided to speak from the heart.

Sharing the truth was difficult, and never more so than when I wrote of the great disappointment surrounding my Lions Tour 2009 experience. Selection for this elite squad had been a dream realised; the suspension preventing my involvement in the tour the stuff of nightmares. I had gone from elation to devastation, and the time period that followed was one of the bleakest I've known. It was a disappointment, that, logically, I knew I simply had to deal with, but dealing with knockbacks when you're already feeling anxious? Not so easy!

Red-Blooded revealed my relationship with depression and anxiety. It exposed the undercurrents beneath my success-ful sporting career, and lifted the lid on that macho image. The media picked up on the story big time, which led to fur-ther attention. And so, unintentionally, I became the 'go-to' guy for interviews on the subject of depression!

Speaking the truth turned out to be one of the best decisions I have ever made. Since my book's release, I have spent a considerable amount of time discussing my personal experiences, sharing them with young people and organisations working in the area of mental health. I have found this hugely stimulating: not only has it gone some small way towards breaking taboos surrounding mental health issues, it has also been massively helpful to me. I am now very aware of how I am predisposed to feel, and why that is. I concentrate on controlling what I can, and do my utmost to ignore what is beyond my control. I think about choices, and try to make the healthier, happier ones. I am the person, remember, who wouldn't tell my parents what was going on; now I stand up in front of crowds of strangers and give them the whole nine yards!

I am stronger, much stronger, for it. I've realised that what people might think of me doesn't matter – it's how we all think about ourselves, how we mind our mental health, that does.

Everybody has a negative voice in there, telling them they can't do stuff. Before, if I had a day off I might just go back to bed and wallow. I'd be lying there, worrying, but doing nothing. So now I almost force myself to get out and go for a walk, meet a friend for lunch, or play a round of golf. I make plans that will keep me out in the world and amongst people, rather than spending too much time alone, letting negative thought patterns build up. I try to be in the here and now, to stay on top of my emotions, and I train my brain, just as I would my body.

In sport and life, practise is the key to success. If you can identify with the feeling that there is a washing machine constantly spinning in your head, you need to practise methods of switching it off, or slowing it down at least. I still have days when I wake up feeling anxious, when I'm aware that the washing machine is spinning too quickly. This awareness allows me to stop and think: what steps can I take to slow the machine down? Are there any small issues I can sort out today, rather than blocking them out until they escalate? Do I need a break?

Now don't get me wrong: pressure is a part of life, and pressure is a positive force when managed well. It is stimulating, encouraging you to work hard to achieve goals. With zero pressure we might all fall out of the bed in the morning and not bother getting off the floor. But I see too many young people, too many people in business, pushing and pushing themselves to achieve, sacrificing their mental health in the process.

The solution is downtime. We all need it. My new career as a sports analyst and writer sees me dealing with pressurised situations such as live television, and my schedule has become more erratic than ever before. If I have a day off, my natural inclination is to worry that I'm not doing enough, to feel guilty about that downtime and so I need to remind myself regularly that downtime is a requirement, that switching off is something I need to do in order to be happy. And guess what? I'm starting to really look forward to my days off.

What I have learned, ultimately, is that it's never a bad idea to open up. Honesty and vulnerability are strengths, and there are loads of brilliant people out there who are only too willing to help you. Don't feel like spilling out all your fears and worries to your friends? That's okay: you can find someone a little bit older who will listen to you, someone who will reassure you that feeling down sometimes is okay, too. That's what becoming aware of your mental health is: thinking, learning and, most importantly, talking about it.

Good mental health also needs fuel. That will come from eating well, minimising alcohol consumption, taking regular exercise and trying, if you can, not to be so hard on yourself. It also comes from the recognition that negativity is a facet of life, but that we have the power to choose how much negativity we are willing to absorb.

If I could leave you with one piece of advice it would be this: focus on finding and celebrating your true value in life. We all have value. Some people are great academically, others are brilliant with their hands, others again are fantastic with people. Everyone has something, and we should all learn to be proud of the unique skills we bring to the world. So take it easy, take time to nurture your true value, and take it from me: happiness is yours for the taking.

Suzanne Byrne

The story of my mental health isn't an epic one. It's much more about everyday trials and tribulations, the things that make you question who you are and what you are here for. My mental health story is purely to do with getting my head around my own self-worth. It's not about the effects others have had on me, circumstances I've been dealt, or society's prejudices. It is simply about one young woman's opinion of herself.

At the moment I consider my mental health to be in reasonably good shape. I mostly put this down to being very aware of myself, and also to coming to terms with who I am. Beyond that, it's about valuing me just for being me.

I've never been one of those 'just naturally talented' people. I had to work hard in school for average results. I tried so many sports and instruments growing up; I enjoyed them all but never excelled at any of them. Besides the constant hobby-hopping, I was a very well-behaved teen. I don't think I ever gave my parents or teachers anything to worry about. I always had good friends, got involved in whatever was going on, got fine exam results. I was perfectly average in many ways, and that's precisely what bothered me. Feeling average made me feel inadequate. It made me feel like I had something huge to prove to the world.

As far as I could see, I was surrounded by amazing people: A-students, athletes or musicians. I remember always being on the bench for the basketball team, being a back-up on the quiz team, being in the chorus of the choir. Looking back I don't think these are a big deal individually or even collectively. When I was 15, however, they were a massive deal and they completely affected the way I viewed myself.

Was there one momentous life event that made me suddenly appreciate who I am? I don't think so, but if I were to try to pick out a key change in my life it would have to be transition year in secondary school. I had changed schools after the Junior Cert. That change was the best decision I ever made.

My new school opened up a world of new opportunities and experiences. I had a whole new network of friends who were easy-going and drama-free. I loved every minute of that year. The change in environment made me realise that it's only when you decide to remove yourself from a situation that you can appreciate how toxic the previous one had been. Change is difficult and unnerving but the outcomes can be wonderful.

I embraced every new opportunity around me and with these new experiences I felt quite empowered and enriched. It broadened my understanding of what education and skills are, and what they mean. Suddenly, I found myself with loads of amazing new things to be involved in. I began developing skills in organisation and event planning, which I've taken into my adult and professional life.

Understanding and valuing who I am was, and is, a process. I don't think anyone wakes up one morning and magically has amazing self-esteem. I did – and still do – go through peaks and troughs with it. Let's face it: despite the miracle of GHDs we all have bad hair days every now and again. The biggest change for me in the last twelve years is that now, when I have those bad days, I don't try to shake them off or deny them. Instead I indulge them. I watch ridiculously cheesy television or movies and allow myself to be okay with feeling a bit crap. Vitally, I know that those bad feelings will go away again.

I have wonderful friends and an even better family. This is hugely important and I truly believe that by being able to talk things through with them was more than half the battle. Talking works, but at the end of the day I know that you somehow find a way to become comfortable in your own skin. For me, a decision to stop comparing myself to other people formed a big part of that process. Comparison is part of the human condition. I think most people probably had at least one person in school they compared themselves to. Letting go of comparisons was tough, but again it was a gradual process. It still is, if I'm honest, and I often have to remind myself that I can't control other people, but I can control my own actions in this moment – and that is a brilliant and powerful thing.

Stephen Daunt

If you want to live life to the full you're going to have to take risks. You'll probably have to ignore people too, the type of people who go, 'What? You can't do that!'

I learnt this pretty early in life. I didn't feel the need to walk until I was seven. The medical professionals told my family I would probably never walk. One day – I can't remember when – I just got up and wobbled around. It must have been after my First Holy Communion as my schoolteachers remember I was carried up to the altar in somebody's arms.

Taking risks

Fast-forward to the rough and tumble of secondary school. It was a tough comprehensive on the wrong side of the tracks, but like all schools they did school trips. The idea of Paris in the spring struck a chord with the 14-year-old me. There was just one thing: in the lifetime of the school not one disabled student had asked to go on a trip.

Don't hold back

I was fine. A wheelchair was found so I didn't need to walk. Paris was ticked off the bucket list. The travel bug was introduced into my body. A few years later, I talked a friend into InterRailing around Europe for a month. This time there was no wheelchair. We walked around twelve European cities and took overnight trains to recover. For a person who loves travel, it was an amazing ride. It was just after the Berlin Wall had fallen so it was amazing to walk through that historic city trying to figure out whether you were in the East or the West. After two weeks, the train pulled into Venice. Talk about a life-affirming moment. When the train pulls in, you still think you are in a normal city but then you walk out of the station and see the Grand Canal. It is a memory seared into my brain and its sheer beauty inspires me every time I think of it.

Journalism was always something I wanted to do. Along the way I was sidetracked and became the first member of my family to go to Trinity. What did I do? Well, two bits of paper say I have a BA and an M.Litt in English but mostly I hung out in the drama society where a few plays were directed and a few parties were attended.

There was one occupational therapist who looked at me with horror when I said that journalism was for me. Are you insane, boy? You only type with one finger.

I wonder whether she's reading this?

It took a few years but I can now call myself a journalist. There were lots of twists and turns along the way. Don't be afraid of these twists and turns. They can take you on journeys you could have never have imagined. Don't be afraid of them. You have your whole life in front of you. I was 40 years old before I got inside the Newstalk door. This was after I had done time in the voluntary sector, as well as courses, back-to-work schemes, and all manner of other stuff. I was lucky that I stayed positive. How? I enjoyed what I was doing. I also never gave up. This might be easier said than done but please DO have dreams. Think big but have fun at the same time. Life is one big banana skin so you might slip on it once in a while, but keep going. You will get there.

Along the way I've had an incredibly loving family, a great set of friends and now a really amazing bunch of work colleagues who put up with my flights of fancy and decisions to try things that I really shouldn't do. That's called love. They love me and I love them. It sounds simple but love is an incredible thing. People love you. Never forget that.

Louise McSharry

When I was growing up, I got really good at being new. I attended eight different schools over the course of my education, thanks to my family's penchant for moving, and in each school I had a different identity. In my first school I was the Irish girl who spoke with a funny accent, in the second school I was the girl who never had the cool clothes, in the third I was the girl who tried and failed to get onto the student council. I was never really the 'cool' girl, but I wanted to be.

I did my very best to become someone who would be respected and admired by my peers in every school I went to. I knew I wasn't going to be the prettiest, so I just tried to be the best at other things. I wanted to be the best actress, so I auditioned for every school play. I wanted to be the best singer so I practised and practised and practised in the hope that I would be good enough for a choir solo. It never really happened, though, and by the time I got to my eighth and final school I was a little weary from all my efforts.

I joined the school in fifth year, having not attended an Irish school for the nine previous years. I didn't really understand how things worked, but I did my best to feign familiarity. One of the prettiest, most popular girls in my year was asked to look after me for the first couple of days, and I did my very best to connect with her and her friends. It kind of worked. I managed to get an invitation to a cool party, and hung out on the periphery of that group for a good while, but in truth I was never part of it. As the year went on I found other friends, people I had more in common with, and people I was more comfortable with. It was a relief not to have to make an effort, to be honest. Not to have to be on high alert all the time, looking for the opportunity to contribute something worthwhile to a conversation I wasn't really into in order to get approval from a group who didn't really get me. It was great to laugh over silly things, and talk about music with people who were into the same things I was. It was so nice to be with people like me.

I was still friendly with the 'popular crowd', or whatever silly name those groups are given, and there were a few girls I really liked, so when an optional school trip came around I decided at the last minute that I'd go. One of the 'popular' girls suggested it, and it sounded like fun so I thought, 'Why not?'

Later that day, word got back to me that not everyone thought my attendance was a good idea. Apparently one of the 'cool girls' had been making unkind remarks in maths. Something along the lines of, 'Well, if Louise is going I don't think I want to go'. I heard this second-hand from one of the girls who was there. It stung at first, but then she told me that the other people in the class, lads and girls, had all responded in a way that surprised me. According to my friend, they had all told the girl in question to shut up, told her that she was being a sap, and that there was nothing wrong with me. Suddenly I realised that there *was* nothing wrong with me. The problem was hers. Her insecurity, her need to feel better about herself. It wasn't about me at all.

Predictably, the girl in question soon heard that I knew about her remarks. Perhaps out of genuine regret, or perhaps because they hadn't gone down very well, she approached me in the corridor between classes to apologise.

'I know you heard what I said in maths,' she said. 'I'm really sorry, it was stupid.'

'It's fine,' I replied, cool as a cucumber.

'Really?' she said, 'That's very good of you.'

And here I had my moment. Perhaps my first totally honest and genuine exchange with a 'popular girl' in that school – I smiled and said, 'You know what? The thing is, I'd probably be really upset if I cared what you thought of me but the truth is, I really don't. So you can say and think whatever you like about me, but I'm not going to care.'

Because, suddenly, I didn't care. Why was I wasting my time trying to get these people who I didn't even like to like me? In that moment, everything was clear.

I'd love to say that that was the end of me trying to impress people who were never really going to be my friends. Unfortunately it wasn't. However, over the years those efforts decreased bit by bit, and now it's rare that I find myself in that position, and let me tell you, it is fantastic. Maybe I've finally become the girl I had a glimpse of in that school corridor in fifth year.

Darragh Doyle

I wrote this for the child I may one day have. I hope he or she will read it and enjoy it. I wrote this because I wish I'd read something similar when I was young. I'm glad I've learned these lessons as I got older. I continue to learn these lessons every day. It's only now I'm doing something about that.

Life isn't always easy or fun or interesting or nice, but it has potential. You'll need to learn to recognise that, deal with it and/or accept and challenge it. Each piece of advice may not be exactly right for you or for anyone else, but if it helps one person like it has helped me, then that's great.

Try to be happy.

You don't need to be happy all of the time. You don't need to be happy even some of the time. Just don't be happy only once upon a time. Every day try to find something, to do something, to go somewhere and to talk to someone that will make you happy.

Try to be happy.

Read. Read funny writings. Read interesting books. Read beautiful poetry. Look for inspiration. Read about other cultures. Read about other countries. Read about science. Read about biology. Read about health. Read about people. Read stories. Read plays. Read poetry aloud. Read *If*, read 'Desiderata', read Rumi, read Pratchett, read Shakespeare, read Yeats, read Frost, read Braley, read Seuss, read Ghigna, read Ingoldsby, read Google. Find things. Love books. Love words. Never stop learning.

Dress well. Find clothes that fit you and suit you. Find clothes you're comfortable in. Dress every day like you're going to meet the love of your life. Look at yourself in the mirror before you leave the house. Don't brush your teeth after you've put on a tie. A well-tailored suit is something to keep well. Mind your clothes. Be clean. Be well presented. People like that.

Be kind. The world is not kind, but you can be. Look at people when they're talking to you. Learn to listen and to let others tell their stories. Learn to empathise. Give generous tips to people who are serving you. Donate to charities. Organise fundraisers. Spend time with old people. Talk to children as young people. Talk to homeless people not because they are homeless, but because they are people. Ask people how they are and listen to the answer. Spend time with people who want to spend time with you. Not everyone is nice, but you can be.

Dance. Even if it's just in your bedroom on your own, or in the kitchen to the radio. Move your body in whatever way you can. A lot of dance is just the confidence to enjoy the music and the movement. Stretch. Shake your bum. Move your arms. Have fun. It's pretty much the same for singing. SING. Every day, sing something. Sing something happy if it's in your heart to.

Try to be happy.

Work. Work at something you're interested in, something that will make your world a better place. Don't live to work – work to live. If you can get paid for it, even better. Don't do nothing all the time. Value your time and your skills and what you can give people. Take pride in what you do and do it well. Help other people in your work but get what you have to do done. Remember, the world at large is very needy and really only cares about what it can get from you, so be happy with what you give and don't expect gratitude, but always welcome thank yous. You will fail sometimes but at least you tried. Learn from that. Avoid complacency, strive for better than mediocrity and realise that problems are opportunities. What you do doesn't have to make money, but if it benefits people and the world, it will benefit you.

Create. Every day, try to do something creative. Write. Draw. Cook. Paint. Plant. Doodle. Compose. Experiment. Colour. Make something that marks your day, be that a poem, a drawing, a tidier garden or a good plate of beans on toast. Even if it's small, it's still something.

Travel. See the world. Talk to locals. Ask for advice. Walk. Go to arts, cultural and sporting events. Experience different cultures by respectfully joining in. Try to pronounce words. Learn friendly useful phrases. Don't be afraid to ask for help. A smile is pretty much the same in every language.

Eat. Drink. Enjoy food. Learn to cook. Don't eat or drink to excess, but realise also that food and drink are fuel for your body. Research food, research nutrition. Try new foods. Eat sushi. Try noodles. Try seafood. Try something exotic. Go for picnics. Cook for others. Give up alcohol at least once in a while – it'll make the next first sip a little better than your last one.

Try to be happy.

Accept. People are different to you and that's okay. The world isn't always a nice place and that's okay. You won't be happy all the time and that's okay. People won't always be polite, considerate, compassionate or kind. Work won't always be fulfilling or interesting. Money will be tight, the weather will be bad and life will be difficult. These things happen. Learn how to accept and deal with them. Don't judge anyone for their lifestyle choices, for how they were born or for how they live their lives – if you don't want to be around them, don't be. Accept but challenge your own limitations.

Challenge. There are things you can change, most of all yourself, your mindset and your problems. Do that. Try to improve things for yourself and for the people you love and who love you. If you can improve the situation, fix the problem or make things better, try to. Challenge yourself with learning something new, with exploring somewhere new, with new situations, new people and new ideas. Leave everywhere you go a little better.

Exercise. Move. Stretch. Walk. Jog. Dance. Run. Lift. Hobble. Crawl. Whatever your abilities, your capabilities or your situations, treat your body with respect and make it stronger and fitter with a bit of exercise. Don't do it to look good for others. Do it to feel good about yourself.

Find friends. They don't have to be people you grew up with, people you work with, people you're introduced to, people in the same country as you or people who look the same as you; they do, however, have to be people who want the best for you, who share interests with you and who you enjoy spending time with. There's a big difference between being friendly with people and being friends with them. Be more considerate of the latter. You're never as alone as you think you are.

Try to be happy.

Want. Learning the difference between what you need and what you want is something you may not like to do but when you learn the difference it's very liberating. You'll find there's actually lots you don't need, so you can enjoy getting the things you want. Fulfil your needs, find out what you really want and go for it. Enjoy getting it.

Think. Learn at first to understand so you can be understood. Evaluate your experiences, your situations, your problems and your opportunities. Try to understand what you're up to and why. Imagine. Visualise. Pretend. Dream. Believe. Examine. Ask.

Talk. As much as listening is important and compassion a skill to cultivate, talking is also something you should always do. Tell stories. Tell jokes. Do things to have something to talk about and please, please, *please* talk about your problems. If you're feeling sad, down, scared or unable to cope, talk to someone about it. It doesn't have to be a loved one you talk to. Go to a doctor. Go to a counsellor. Go to someone and talk to them. You won't be happy all the time but keeping sadness inside won't help either. There is always someone who has had a similar or worse problem – talk to them and see what they did to overcome it. Search the internet. Talk online. Talk in person. Just talk.

Love. It sounds simple, but really isn't. Love yourself if you can. Love other people. Love the place you live in and love what you do. Realise they won't always love you. Enjoy falling in love. Enjoy being in love. Enjoy being single. Enjoy the possibility that you'll be in love. Enjoy sex but never have sex if you don't want it and never have sex with someone who doesn't want it as much as you. Love love.

Try to be happy.

Try. My last one, my child, and the most important. Try. Try something new, try something strange, try something difficult, try something interesting, try something fun. Try getting out of bed in the morning. Try looking well before you leave the house. Try being on form and in a good mood for the day. Try being nice to people. Try eating well. Try enjoying what you do. Try talking to people. Try learning a skill. Try a new word. Try to create something. Try not to fail but if you do, try again. Try to work on why you're not happy. Try to change things for the better. Try to be happy.

I do. I did. I am. When I do, I am. When I try, I do. Do try. Try to be happy.

Activity

List little things that make you happy ...

Today

Something I learned ...

Something that pleasantly surprised me ...

An act of kindness witnessed ...

Something beautiful ...

Something I am grateful for ...

Three experiences that have helped shape the person I am today ...

Choose your own adventure. Pick one of these to make happen within the next month:

Go on a day trip to somewhere you've always wanted to visit

Write someone a letter telling them how much they mean to you

Try mindfulness or mediation

Create a playlist of songs that make you happy

Write your own mental health adventure:

BIOGRAPHIES

Suzanne Byrne

Suzanne lives in Inchicore but will always be a north Dub at heart. She loves travelling to new places and says her favourite place in the world is Lake Malawi as the sunsets are fab. Suzanne got involved with ReachOut.com in 2011 and her work with ReachOut.com's Youth Advisory Network inspired her to continue working with young people. She now works with young people in Comhairle na nÓg youth councils around the country as a Participation Officer and loves it to bits. Suzanne sent us this picture to accompany her story and said, 'This picture makes me happy because I'm attached to one of the two parachutes. The other parachute is my boyfriend Gary. It makes

me happy because it was such an adventure and although I was scared out of my wits, I did it and was really proud of myself.'

Melissa Maria Carton

Melissa currently works as an actress and a writer for Chunk.ie. Born, raised and currently residing in The Liberties, Dublin, Melissa loves travelling, finding a bargain on sale and family days out. She dislikes trying to get through crowds when town is busy and she has to get somewhere, and 5 a.m. starts. She claims that if left in a room on her own for too long, she will start chatting to herself. She reveals that she would love to write and publish a book of her own someday and that she also enjoys reading, writing, going for long walks and photography.

In explaining why she wanted to contribute to this book, Melissa said, 'When I was going through a dark time I didn't feel like I could tell anyone. I felt like people would tell me I was exaggerating my problems, that they wouldn't understand, that they wouldn't want to be my friend if I was suffering from depression so I wanted to let the readers of this book know that they are not alone. Everyone has bad times. No one is perfect. If you feel like you can't cope with the feelings you're having, the best thing to do is tell someone. The people who love you would rather you lean on them for support than see anything bad happen to you, so let them know how you're feeling. I wish I had spoken up sooner about how I was feeling at the time. Know that you don't have to go through it all on your own. There are people who can and want to help you.'

Oliver Clare

A long-distance runner and blogger, Oliver ran his first race in aid of ReachOut.com back in March 2012 and is currently sitting pretty on twenty-five marathons. By day, he works in accounts and by night can be found entertaining strangers at any karaoke bar that will let him in. He's also a politics nerd with a penchant for *West Wing* reruns, and can often be found attempting to string a sentence or two together at www.runningforreachout.ie or @OliverClare on Twitter.

Caitrina Cody

Caitrina has lived in London for almost two years, working as a free-lance copywriter and editor. Caitrina explained why she wanted to con-tribute to this book by saying, 'I feel very lucky to be part of this book – I've admired the work of ReachOut. com since I worked on one of their campaigns back in 2011. I love read-ing and writing, and it's my goal to one day write a book I can be really proud of from start to finish, even if nobody else gets to read it.'

Amy Colgan

Amy is from Dublin but is currently living in Brussels, home of waffles, beer, and people who wear very round spectacles. She works in communications, or 'writing things' as she puts it. When she first left college, she had the opportunity

to work for ReachOut.com on a campaign that took her all over the country and gave her an incredible chance to talk to hundreds of people about being young in Ireland, about their friends and their community. Amy feels this experience showed her how many inspiring people there are out there, with big ideas and big hearts.

Things Amy loves are: tea, buttery toast, epic conversations about saving the world, having friends all over the globe. Amy is currently learning to ride a bicycle (again).

Brendan Courtney

Brendan Courtney has achieved so many things it's tricky to know where to start. He's a TV presenter who's fared incredibly well in Ireland and the UK, a writer, broadcaster, fashion stylist, and – yep! – a fashion designer too. In the last year, this bright spark of positive energy has released a second book, opened a fashion boutique, and – also in cahoots with his partner and best

pal Sonya Lennon – has launched FrockAdvisor, an innovation in how we shop online. Meet Brendan and you'd be forgiven for believing he is always blissfully happy, always looking ahead, and has probably lived a life utterly devoid of fear or self-doubt. Here's the truth, though: he's been through ups, downs and in-betweens, just like every one of the rest of us.

Elaine Crowley

Cork native Elaine Crowley earns her living from talking. She's both the presenter and producer (trust us; this makes her exceptional) of top-rating TV show *Midday* on TV3. This means she needs to be ready to lead a discussion on just about any subject – from religion to the *Rose of Tralee* – live in front of the nation, every single day. Elaine is known for the courage of her convictions; her open dialogue on the subject of mental health is testament to this trait. She talks about the importance of 'baby steps' here.

Stephen Daunt

Describing himself as 'Bon Vivant' and 'Vodka Drinker', journalist Steve Daunt has worked with Newstalk radio station for seven years, where he acts as a researcher for the Lunchtime show and writes a bi-weekly blog. He's a travel addict with a BA and M.Lit in English from Trinity College Dublin, who also has Cerebral Palsy. Daunt by name; undaunted by nature, as his piece, rewritten for us by Steve from an original Newstalk broadcast, proves ...

Sinéad Desmond

If Sinead Desmond has an 'off' button, we have yet to find it. She's the woman up *before* the lark every day, jumping out of bed at 4 a.m. to make her way to the *Ireland AM* studio, where she co-anchors Ireland's most popular breakfast TV show. Her life motto is 'the harder you work, the luckier you get', and based on her career we're gonna start getting up earlier, stat. But Sinead's learned the importance of healthy balance, too: her spare time spent sailing, scuba diving and talking long walks with her golden retriever, Jack. Mental health recently took on new meaning for Sinead, as she explains here.

June Devaney

June states she 'wears too many hats'. Although not always stylish, she claims they have been created by some of the most influential designers in her life. They sport labels such as; 'Motherhood', 'Passionate Student', 'Social Activism', 'Human Rights', 'Lawyer-in-the-Making', 'Concert-Chaser', 'Cupcake Lover', 'Writer', 'Reader', 'Artist', 'Hailing From Mayo' and 'NO to Scratchy Towels'.

June first became involved with ReachOut.com through various networks while working in the mental health field. She explains how ReachOut.com helped her when she needed guidance with a project, and in return she helped ReachOut.com by writing stories for the website about her experiences of dealing with, and getting through personal challenges, using such experiences to support others and to create wider social change.

Darragh Doyle

Darragh Doyle (@darraghdoyle) is a Social Media Strategy and Community Manager who uses the internet to tell people about events and ideas and to share images, videos and very bad jokes that make people's days better. He works on Irish events, film, television, theatre and tourism projects.

Working on great projects for RTÉ, Riverdance, Heartbeat of Home, Sony Pictures, 20th Century Fox and the City Spectacular Festival, as well as managing the @ireland project, helping the London Irish Centre and promoting Irish events around the world, Darragh keeps himself and others busy, informed and entertained.

He is passionate about positivity, proud of Ireland and Irish people worldwide and believes anything he can do, you can do better. And yes, he does have a blue nose in real life, but only one or two weekends a year. Find him online and ask him why.

Emma Hannigan

The word 'survivor' doesn't even cut it for Emma Hannigan. She's a mum, an author and an activist – if an accidental one. Y'see, Emma has beaten cancer eight times, and has learned that writing down her experiences bolstered the strength required to keep on fighting. The byproduct, her many best-selling books, has not only provided her with solace in dark times, it's shed light on that most frightening of diseases for thousands of others. Emma's message is that looking to the future, even when a future itself is in doubt, is imperative. Here she shares her story, life skills and hard-won wisdom.

Vicky Kavanagh

Vicky Kavanagh is a journalist and writer. Aged 23, she lives on the Northside of Dublin with a cat named Beau. She loves books, old movies, Soap & Glory products, brunch on Sundays and thirty-second dance parties.

Katie Kelly

Katie likes to write, read, and be with her friends 'who are all amazing'. She studied media and creative writing, and adores all things from the '90s and festivals. She loves techno, hates Dubstep and when things become difficult, she always tries to remember to – 'Keep on keeping on!'

Ian Lacey

From Gorey, Co. Wexford, Ian now lives in Laos, Southeast Asia where he writes for a travel magazine. He became involved with ReachOut. com in 2010 working with their volunteer network and saw the incredible power young people's voices have encouraging positive mental health. When not writing, he can be found plotting the most interesting and colourful bicycle route back home!

Rosemary McCabe

Fingers in pies; that's Rosemary's thing. And yes, sometimes these fingers are in actual pies (this is very usual for a writer working from home), but mainly they're poking around in professional-type confections. Rosemary is the girl from school who did 'really well' – you know the one, and you know she deserves every bit of her success too. Rosemary's bagged a whole load of dream jobs as proof, from fashion writing for *The Irish Times* to style opining on Frillseeker.ie. We love her tweets, her features and her at-times brutal candour, but mainly we're waiting for her to write a book, which we'll be the first to buy.

Eoghan McDermott

Eoghan found national fame through a backstage present-ing slot on *The Voice of Ireland*, and you can tune in to his break-fast show every Saturday and Sunday morning on 2fm. You may also have spotted him doing the 'Ice Bucket Challenge' in a tutu. A blue one. Here he shares what happened when he decided it was time to make a little confession.

Louise McSharry

You could say Louise McSharry stood out from the crowd from the start. She was, after all, crowned the Heinz/Woman's Way Baby of the Year 1984. Rather than rest on her laurels, however, 31-year-old Louise has since gone on to forge a kickass career in broadcasting – when writing this piece for us she was filling in for Ryan Tubridy on 2fm, in addition to her regular show every evening. She's also the founder of the fabulous Fanny.ie, and recommends listening to Taylor Swift – loud – when life throws you a curveball.

Tara Ní Mhóráin

You know that phrase about someone lighting up a room once they walk into it? That's Tara Ní Mhóráin to a tee. She's one of the sunniest person- alities we've ever come across, bursting with positivity and always ready to help someone else out – usually ahead of her- self! Tara recently completed an MA in Irish translation at DCU; making her one smart cookie who also happens to dig a great Disney movie. Her story will resonate with anyone who's moved away from home, or is missing someone now living in a foreign land.

Thomas Noonan-Ganley

Thomas lives in Dublin. He works part-time with ReachOut.com and part-time in a shop (which breaks his heart, but it pays the bills). He likes peanut butter, marmite and yoga, though not necessarily together.

He spends his spare time day-dreaming about the future, socialising, and trying to master the head-stand. He's not there yet, but will persevere.

Sheila O'Flanagan

Does pinning down your perfect career seem impossible? Don't worry: if you're anything like Sheila O'Flanagan life's twists and turns will take you where you need to be. Sheila was one of Ireland's leading financial dealers; the first woman to run the trading department of an Irish commercial bank. She was good – really good – at her job, but what bothered her was all that moving of money around rather than actually *creating* anything. So, she bit the bullet: sitting down to write her first book in her mid-thirties. Fast forward to today and Sheila recently passed best-selling book number twenty-five, and is one of Ireland's most successful authors – ever! She took time out to write this short piece on the perils of comparison.

Louise O'Neill

Things Louise O'Neill loves: her family, her dog Jinky, yoga and reading. Things she doesn't: society's forced ideals of how girls 'should' look and behave – well, that's the main thing really. Louise studied English and History at Trinity College before taking on a post-grad in Fashion Buying and Management at DIT. From there, to New York, where she worked at *Elle* magazine: surrounding herself with high fashion and A-List celebs, and finding her high fashion colleagues were pretty lovely people, actually. She returned to Ireland in 2011 and her first book, *Only Ever Yours*, is now a critically-acclaimed best-seller, which Louise hopes young women 'will read and think maybe what they've been told about the way women have to be and act isn't 100 per cent true'.

Aisling O'Toole

Aisling is many things: a brilliant writer, editor (of *Irish Country Magazine*), broadcaster and recently-qualified yoga teacher. But what she is above all? HONEST! Aisling has never been afraid to tell it like it is, a fact even she finds surprising at times. She likes nothing better than a very large conversation over a similarly-sized glass of wine, and there is no better woman for an inspiring piece of advice ... or a quote you'll want to stick to the palm of your hand (follow her @toolelebon for evidence).

Harriet Parsons

Harriet Parsons is a psycho-therapist and the services coordinator with Bodywhys, The Eating Disorders Association of Ireland. This is very different from where Harriet started out. When she was 16 years old, she went to Perm, in Russia, to study ballet. Having graduated and worked with the Chelyabinsk Opera and Ballet theatre, Harriet joined Moscow City Ballet and toured Germany and the UK. In 1998, Harriet hung up her ballet shoes and went to college to study psychology. This was a major life change, and it took some time to get used to sitting in a lecture hall rather than standing in the wings warming up for a performance. Harriet has now been with Bodywhys for nine years, and loves her work, as you can see by the piece she has written for this book. Life is for living, she says, there are ups and downs, but this is what makes it exciting!

Eoin Pluincéid

Eoin is a teacher based in Kildare, who enjoys photography and touring Ireland. He cooks to relax, and would rather fight one hundred duck-sized horses than one horse-sized duck.

Alan Quinlan

Rugby legend Alan Quinlan is a former Ireland backrow and lock who played twenty-seven times for his country, including at two World Cups. He was also a shining light of the Munster squad, with whom he won the Heineken Cup on two occasions. Alan was long seen as the epitome of the macho Irish man, causing surprise to many in 2012 when he publicly revealed his long battle with depression and anxiety. One of the first sporting figures to open up about mental health, he now supplements his work as a sports journalist and broadcaster with a serious amount of time spent promoting his positive message. He shares his mental health story and practical advice here.

Steve Wall

Not content with one impressively creative career, Clare-born Steve Wall has recently returned to acting. Currently playing Einar in *Vikings* series 2, January 2015 will see his starring role in BBC's *Silent Witness* hit screens, while we're still watching his hilarious turn on Sky's *Moone Boy* on repeat. Irish music fans will know him as the lead singer of both The Stunning and The Walls, with whom he has entertained the masses both at home and across the world for close on a quarter of a century. He's not focussing on the timeframe, though – as every new experience brings him right back to square one. This is Steve's take on what life's scarier moments have taught him.

Laura Whitmore

Laura's career in TV began in 2008 when she won the 'MTV Pick Me' competition which led to her becoming the key face of MTV EUROPE. She has worked for all the major broadcasters and is the hugely popular host of ITV2's *I'm A Celebrity Get Me Out Of Here Now*. When she is not travelling around the world interviewing the biggest names in music and film or presenting from the jungle, Laura is also in-demand on the fashion and beauty circuit as well as being an in demand DJ for live events.

Laura likes to knit and is an avid baker. She has an unhealthy obsession with smelly cheese, Stinking Bishop blue cheese being her favourite. Her best dance move is 'the robot'.

AFTERWORD

To everyone who has written or read a piece in this collection, thank you. The generous contributions to this book have made me feel humble, inspired, happy, sad and most of all, grateful. I'm grateful for the existence in this world of the people who have shared a part of themselves through this book. Sharing is a two-way thing, and the greater purpose of sharing everyday adventures in mental health is to open doors, start conversations, make cultural change, give courage, and instil belief.

When we started the ReachOut.com journey in Ireland five years ago our mission was to help young people live happier lives. We started off excited and confident that what we were doing would matter and that we could make a difference. Since then, through the positive response of everyone we have been able to share our ever evolving worldview with, we know we are making a difference.

Our mission, now, is to work with all of you to make sure that the gaze of mental health is extended. Mental health is not about the one in four, it's about all of us. Mental health, for better or worse, is a part of all of us every day, shaping our activities, guiding our interaction with each other, influencing our optimism or fuelling our fears. Our mental health is expressed when we're on the dancefloor, pedalling a bicycle, performing our jobs, doing exams, arguing, hugging, writing, despairing, rejoicing, just being.

Just as mental health is part of each of us and is played out all the time in everyday settings, so do we have a fundamental right to claim expertise in it. Our mental health is not an abstract neurological plain but a reflection of the things that happen in the world around us. You understand and know more about your mental health than you might think. Trust yourself, know yourself and you will able to look after your mental health better. One of the best ways any of us can get to know ourselves better is by sharing stories. I once heard an Olympic athlete tell a conference room full of teenagers, in a very matter of fact way, that nobody ever regrets having done some physical exercise. I hope that none of our story-tellers have any regrets after the mental exercise of telling their story.

Our relationship with mental health tells a lot about how we identify as human beings. Are we merely biological beings whose functions and malfunctions are more or less predictable and logical? Or are we more than that? At a time of greater religious uncertainty when many of us are searching for meaning or are reconciling ourselves with the lack of meaning in life, there is real power and real strength to be drawn from other people, and other people's stories. Our everyday adventures in mental health shine a light on our shared humanity and can bring us together like nothing else.

Derek Chambers
ReachOut.com